As "I" See It
The Scientifically Spiritual Perspective

As "I" See It
The Scientifically Spiritual Perspective

John Hargreaves

Mulberry Press
Carmel, California

ISBN 0-9645632-2-3

Mulberry Press, Box 461, Carmel, California 93921-0461

In the beginning was One alone;
Seeing nothing but Himself, he said "This is I,"
So "I" became his name forever;
Consequently, to this day, a man thinks of
himself as "I"
And he must be taught some other name,
But to himself he is "I," for that is
the name of the One.
The man said, "Since it is all I, is there anything
to fear from it?"
And the answer from everything was "No,"
For fear can only spring from a second,
And All was One -
So all creation, when they know they
are part of the One, have nothing to fear.
Can you feel fear for yourself? No.
And all is thyself.

From an old legend

Acknowledgements

In writing this book, I have been conscious of the many friends who have offered ideas and, in particular, those both within and without the Christian Science church who have critically and ruthlessly examined what has been written in order to point out gaps and contradictions. If these still appear, it is the fault of the writer and not of them. I would like to include the following by name: Alan Fine, Grace Gordon, Josephine Neil, Jan and Ann Linthorst, Steve Nowlan, and Robert H. B. Wade. Others have contributed their comments and encouragement, and I am grateful to them. And, finally, both the input of ideas and the practical typing support that I have had from my wife have been invaluable.

Table of Contents

Foreword

In 1993, Mulberry Press published a book by John Hargreaves called "The Christian Science Revolution in Thought." This was a distillation of talks he had given over the years to groups of students of Christian Science, and therefore presumed an acquaintance with the writings and language on this subject.

In the year that followed its publication, the first edition was sold out but, during this same period, a large number of requests were received to publish something that would be of interest to the many people who were unbiased searchers for a new answer in this scientific age, and who might or might not be aligned with any faith or organization.

In this new book, the writer introduces three themes which are reiterated throughout. The first is that thinking not only affects, but actually constitutes, experience. The second is that what we are accepting as thought is the standpoint of perception, the "eye," which colours all that is perceived. The third is that the mental framework which characterizes this "eye" is also the identity, the "I," of the beholder.

From this standpoint and framework, the writer suggests a new perspective from which everything can be regarded. He equates this with that altitude of consciousness which, in religious terms, is called the divine Mind, or God. This perspective, in turn, colours everything that is seen from it. The viewpoint determines the view. Thus, the traditional distinction between religious and secular affairs becomes less relevant and gives place to a new fusion in which science and religion, thinking and experience, are found to be aspects of one whole way of living.

In a scientific age, thought finds a new plateau which is neither exclusively religious nor secular but scientifically spiritual. Everything then is seen in a new light, and the answers to contemporary problems are found, not by trying to alter phenomena but by altering the viewpoint from which observation takes place.

Mr. Hargreaves' cultural background has been that of Christian Science, though a wide experience in the course of his various careers has made this background more of a lens through which life is seen than an organisation to which one adheres. This book is not in any way a definitive or comprehensive statement of Christian Science, but rather takes a number of subjects that are of apparent contemporary interest and treats them from the standpoint of the scientific "I." The full exposition of this subject is given by its Discoverer, Mary Baker Eddy, and is set out in her textbook, "Science and Health with Key to the Scriptures." This book can be obtained from Christian Science Reading Rooms and most public libraries throughout the world. "As 'I' See It – The Scientifically Spiritual Perspective" is, at most, an invitation to explore further.

Mr. Hargreaves was born in South Africa and educated in England at Eton. He joined the British Army in World War II, and served as a commissioned officer in the Rifle Brigade in Northwest Europe and, later, in Kenya during the Mau Mau troubles. His military service included periods with Intelligence. He retired from the Army in 1956 and joined IBM United Kingdom, serving for a number of years on its board of directors. In 1976 he took early retirement from IBM and resigned from a number of other directorships,as well as political, educational, and voluntary appointments, to give his full time to the practice of Christian Science. He was first listed as a practitioner in the Christian Science Journal in 1979. Over the years Mr. Hargreaves has contributed many articles to the Christian Science periodicals and has also served on the Christian Science Board of Lectureship. He is a member of First Church of Christ, Scientist in London.

Both the author and the publishers hope that this book will encourage a fresh, non-sectarian, and scientific, rather than just religious, approach to some important questions being raised today.

The Publishers

Editor's Note: Readers may notice that certain words are spelled in two different ways — the British and the American. John Hargreaves uses the British form except when quoting from Mrs. Eddy's writings.

Introduction

When an idea corresponds to the needs
of the times, it is no longer the property
of the man who discovered it, and stronger
than those responsible for it.
                                    Jean Monnet

Today, more than ever, people are seeking some explanation of themselves and their universe which transcends
the merely personal and physical. Their search implies, in
turn, that there can be such an explanation for, to be conscious of it, even as a possibility, one must presume that
it exists. As Pascal said, "Thou could'st not have sought
me, had'st thou not already known me." The questions,
Who am I? What am I? How do I, or should I, relate to
others, to my environment, my universe ? Is there a God,
a prime cause or intelligence — something bigger than
myself? Is there a reason for behaving in a certain way —
a moral law, an absolute Truth? — all these questions are
being asked, tacitly or openly.

It seems clear that the traditional, and often religious,
answers are failing to satisfy, if only because a blind faith
is being challenged by reason and experience. The inability of so-called good people to procure for themselves any
greater tenure of happiness, safety, and freedom than the
so-called bad, has thrown doubt on the efficacy of prayer
and the purpose of worship. The inability of anything
material to offer peace, security, and satisfaction, on any
but a transitory basis, has highlighted the basic dichotomy
between the world of the Spirit and that of Mammon,
without really explaining either. It seems, too often, that
for many who count themselves believers, religion is

something to which one retreats; a realm divorced from what are termed "practical affairs," which neither explains nor embraces the contrasts of daily experience and in which all that is not immediately and rationally explicable is classified as mystery, or worse. That there are wonderful exceptions to this observation does not alter its basic accuracy. As with the Athenians, there would appear to be not just an unknown but an unknowable God.

It is becoming evident that, as is always the case, problems are not solved at the level, or within the terms of reference, of the problem. Until now, these terms of reference have been, in the main, the perception of the physical senses. Accepting the material world as the reality, anyhow for the time being, science has then tried to analyse and explain it; theology has sought to redeem it; and medicine has attempted to patch it up.

But have we really advanced much further or become much wiser? Or have we really only managed to produce as many new problems as those we have explained and solved? At a time of immense crisis in world affairs, there is a growing recognition that there has to be a new approach, a new framework of thought, a new paradigm, as physicists call it. People are realizing that the physical universe, so apparently on the edge of catastrophe, does not contain within itself the solution to its crises. This is why, in increasing numbers, they are seeking an explanation of life that is above the physical — that is, metaphysical — where there can be found a spiritual answer to their questions.

This spiritual answer is to be found at a level of awareness that is higher than the merely personal or humanly mental. It is a level of quality where thought rises above the three-dimensional to the universal reality. Many ascribe the ultimate, and knowable, source of such thought to

Spirit, or God, and accept the explanation and character of everything that proceeds from this source to be spiritual. Throughout this book the term "spiritual" is used to denote that which emanates from this higher source.

Each year in London there is a "Festival of Mind and Body." Many scores of stands focus on a spectrum of subjects that range from meditation to alternate medicine; from dieting to hypnosis; from theosophy to New Age Christianity; from acapuncture to "spiritual" healing, and many other approaches to modern life that the cynic might include under the heading of fads and fancies. But, to do this, would be to miss the point, for it is not the subject matter that thinking people come in their thousands to explore, but the fact that they come! Writing of this event in the London Times, columnist Bernard Levin said, "The offer is not of something outside the individual to be supplied, but of something already inside us, which can be released. They have all come seeking something; something that could give them not certainty (for the belief in that mythical beast died out long ago), but understanding; understanding of themselves and their place in the universe...almost every path on view began in the same place: inside the seeker."

History may seem to repeat itself. It is never static; change is its very nature. Generally the changes take place within an existing set of parameters. For example, the abolition of child labour in Britain was a change that, however desirable, still took place within the traditional framework of master-servant relationships. Only at rare intervals does change become convulsive so that these parameters themselves are challenged.

In what has come to be called a paradigm shift, people seek not just amendments within an existing framework of thought but a change of framework itself; not just an amendment of the rules of the game but a relocation of its goal posts. A new age demands not just revolt against the old but a new and better standpoint of perception. And those who feel they cannot accept this demand, or who have not been told how to rise to it, tend to opt out, drop out, or just become resigned. And, in the last case, they live for today, yet find that today has less and less to offer. They remain in the half-way house, or purgatory, between rebellion and conversion.

My own exploration into a spiritual explanation of the universe began just after World War II, when I was taken out of my regiment in Germany to join the War Crimes Investigation Unit. This entailed finding and interrogating both the staff and the victims of the concentration camps in order to collect depositions to hand over to the legal process of the Nuremberg Trials. It was in the atmosphere of the moral and physical bankruptcy of post-war Europe that I sought some reason for all I was seeing and experiencing. The horrors of the holocaust were fresh in peoples' thought. A mass displacement of populations had caused a near total disintegration of family cohesion and standards. The desperate need to procure the basic essentials of existence overrode any conceivable laws of morality. Revenge, betrayal, and every phenomenon of unleashed animality paraded over the continent. The reaction to these pictures ranged from those whom despair had numbed beyond caring, or those who still believed that expediency could let them take advantage of these conditions a little longer to benefit themselves, to those who still cared and found some faith in a higher power. One of my own discoveries was of a common denominator of character in many of those who had come through the concentration camps with a minimum damage to mind and body. It was that they had ceased to hate. It was not a physical but a moral stamina that prevailed, and some ability to recognise that evil, of whatever dimension, was not personal.

But a basic question remained. If there was a God, let alone one who was Love, how could these things be? My conclusion was that, either they were the responsibility, with whatever purpose, of some underlying cause and intelligence — which seemed unacceptable — or they were unknown to that altitude of thought, of Mind, which itself must transcend the dream of duality called good and evil. Either my kingdom was of this world, with all the enigma that accompanies material existence, or, as Christ Jesus put it, "My kingdom is not of this world."[1] And, if the latter was true, how could this become practical experience, rather than just an escape from an unpleasant and inexplicable environment? While there were some who could not accept any reason behind all they saw and experienced, there were others — many of them — who found in all they had witnessed an inescapable propulsion to seek an explanation that was outside the parameters of that environment and the persons who had suffered in it.

It was within the broad scope of this search that, having enquired into many avenues of religion and philosophy, I retraced some steps that I had taken but discarded as a child, and began to ask about Christian Science. What I now learned made sense, but it came to me, not as a religious sect, nor as a human organization, but as a fundamental law that did govern the universe. It was not one that could come down to human frailty, but rather an unchanging law of good, which was practical in the detail of daily living insofar as we were attuned to it.

Really, everyone has a religion and believes in a God of some sort. The word "religion" stems from the Latin, meaning "to bind back." We all bind back our thinking and behaviour to something. It may be that our sense of

God or good is just expediency. A thief, for example, may believe that what is good for him is obtained by stealing. Another person may make a god, or ruling influence, out of money, or work, or family, or even his or her own intellect. Even the agnostic has to have something about which he is not sure. In every case, what people seek is Truth, or that which fundamentally *is*. The important question is not so much whether there is a God, but *what* is God?

"Science" is another word that concerns us all. Science means "exact knowledge" or understanding. It is inseparable from Truth. Physical sciences refer to the laws of physics. Metaphysics requires a spiritual science to explain it. Mrs. Eddy refers to the discovery of Christian Science in these words: "In the year 1866, I discovered the Christ Science or divine laws of Life, Truth, and Love, and named my discovery Christian Science."[2] And she also writes: "The terms Divine Science, Spiritual Science, Christ Science or Christian Science, or Science alone, she employs interchangeably, according to the requirements of the context. These synonymous terms stand for everything relating to God, the infinite, supreme, eternal Mind."[3] In the context of this book, the term "Spiritual Science" will often be appropriate, because we are looking at a spiritual science, or understanding, of being; an understanding of the spiritual, instead of the physical, laws that govern man and the universe.

Two points can be usefully made. The first is that a discovery is not an invention. Laws are eternal, be they those of physics, hydraulics, or any other science. They antedate their discovery and practical utilization.

The second is that a discovery accompanies understanding, a quality of Mind. A discovery is inseparable from its discoverer but not confined to the discoverer. Contemporary thought failed to understand the teaching and works of Christ Jesus because people thought it was the person, rather than the Principle that he taught and practiced, that did the mighty works. The departure of the personal Saviour relegated the ability to do the same works to the past, and postponed the fulfilment of his promises until the future. And controversy continues to rage over what people see as the person.

In the same way — and whatever impression is sometimes given to the contrary — it is important to recognise that the understanding which discovered, and still discovers, the Spiritual Science of being is not the prerogative of person, but Mind in self-expression. It was not person, but the absence to a unique degree of personal identity, that allowed the vision, greatness, tenderness, and healing power of what appeared as Mary Baker Eddy to shine through and dis-cover, or take the covers off, a Spiritual Science that explains the laws of the universe in spiritual, instead of physical, terms. And her followers love and revere this appearing intelligently only as they share this dis-covery in their own lives; as they let that same Mind discover and explain the Science of Christianity as exemplified by the Master Christian, Christ Jesus. Students who speak of Einstein do so in the context of his prodigious discovery, but it is the discovery that they study and practice. To substitute the study and practice of universal Christian Science with dwelling on the personality of its Discoverer is to deny everything that she taught. "There was never a religion or philosophy lost to the centuries except by sinking its divine Principle in personality."[4]

In my own experience, I found I could accept the discovery and recognise the selflessness and example of its Discoverer. I found that the law of good was effectual, even though I understood little of it. Soon after I began to study, I was taken off to a German hospital with diptheria. I was on the danger list, and my parents were cabled. I had another cable sent to a Christian Science practitioner in England, asking him to pray for me. The next morning, my swabs were negative, and the hospital staff attributed this sudden healing to Christian Science. At the time, I understood little of what had happened — the role of the practitioner, the way prayer worked. I knew only that I was healed, and it was far later, as I began to study seriously, that a real understanding of what had taken place began to dawn.

Since that time, in a busy, varied, and interesting life that has embraced three different careers, this sense of a demonstrable law, in which "all things work together for good to them that love God,"[5] has continued to unfold. But it is always we who have to be in line with the law, and not a law that makes concessions to, or compromises with, human situations. In any science, the requirement is to obey the rules and practice them, because rules cannot be bent to suit human whim. These rules embody a Science, albeit Spiritual, and refer to a way of life, just as early Christianity was known as "the Way." Indeed, with the removal of the misconceptions that get attached to this term, one might suggest that any thinker could be interested in knowing more about this Way and its underlying Science.

The Truth is the centre of all religion. It has to be since, for something to be true, it must be universal and eternal. The purpose of this book is not to advocate yet another approach to the Truth. Nor is the writer equipped to examine the many philosophies or the forms of mental science that are current. In the story of the philosopher who pointed a finger at the moon, it was found that his audience was too absorbed in watching his finger to see the moon. It is only as we get behind the words and forms of the many human approaches to Truth, that we can find Science, or reality. This book grew out of a series of talks to people who came from many traditional backgrounds, and who had come together to discover a commonality of ideas behind the words that had characterised their own particular background and upbringing. The result was not only a unanimity of purpose but also a forum that was totally free of any dissentient element. If this book can help further in removing misconceptions and offer seekers a fresh approach, it will have served its purpose.

1

The Scientific "I"

*Man does not suffer from conditions but
rather from the view he takes of them.*
                                    Epictetus

*Open thou mine eyes that I may behold
wondrous things out of thy law.*
                                    Psalms

The one thing of which anyone can be certain is that I AM.
It is possible to doubt everything that pertains to an external universe — everything that comes to our cognition
through the testimony of the five physical senses, and
everything that relates to another, be it he, she, or they.
But, having discarded everything that might be termed an
unreliable witness to what is really going on, we are still
left with a central conviction which, so far as we are concerned, is beyond question, namely, that I AM. Stronger
than the intellectual statement of Descartes, "I think,
therefore I AM," is the certainty that "because I am conscious, I AM."

We are going to develop the theme that consciousness, not
matter, is the underlying essence of reality, so that knowing and being are found to be one. In a certain sense, we
are our experience, and this leads us to the profound statement by Shakespeare, "There is nothing either good or
bad, but thinking makes it so." Consciousness, as a term,
means more than just thinking, because it is not confined

to the testimony of the physical senses, nor is it just the activity of a human mind. As we shall find later, this consciousness, or spiritual awareness, is ultimately good, and not a mixture of good and evil.

Everything Comes to Us at the Point of Consciousness

While we do not doubt that I AM, we can and do still ask, What am I? If we think about it, when we say "I" we are really referring to our capacity to be aware, to be conscious. Statements such as I know, I hear, or I see, relate to this capacity. It is an entirely mental capacity, because everything comes to us at the point of consciousness. It may be a newscast, the behaviour of another person, a bank statement, or a physical diagnosis, but it is at the point of consciousness that it is received. Were this not so, we should not be aware of it. Only when we become conscious or aware of something can we then identify with it by prefixing the capacity to be aware with the pronoun "I." This means that we deal with everything that comes to us "here" as consciousness, and not "over there" as the phenomenon it appears to be.

Mud and Stars

The reception of all the information that comes to us is, in turn, conditioned by many factors. Two people can receive the same information and "see" or "understand" it in different ways. As the couplet puts it:

> Two men look out through the same bars;
> One sees the mud, and one the stars.

The reason for this is that the capacity to be aware will be influenced by factors such as heredity, upbringing, nationality, education, experience, and so on. These factors form a *mental* framework through which what comes

2

to us is filtered, and by which it is coloured. They determine not just *what* we see, but *how* we see it. Indeed, what "I" see will not only differ from what another may see; it will almost certainly differ from what I used to see, or will see in the future, because the mental reception station will have been amended by further experience.

A Chicken Run

A few years ago, Professor Wilson, a member of the faculty of London University, wrote a paper about the experience of a team of people who went to a remote African village to try to teach the natives about a new method of sanitation. They showed the villagers a film and at the end asked them what they remembered of it. All of them could remember one thing, namely, that a chicken had run across the road at one point. Within their framework of perception, the chicken had some significance, whereas the film of the new sanitary system was so outside their experience that it did not register with them. On the other hand, the people who showed the film noticed the chicken only after the second run. The two frameworks of experience determined what was seen.

Because the capacity to know reflects a mental framework, within which the knowing takes place, it means that, when we say "I," we are really referring to what we accept as mentality, or mind. What I humanly know about myself — my birth, background, schooling, friends, circumstances, successes, failures, hopes and disappointments, good and bad — constitutes what I call my mind, and so to me is what I am. And, of course, my assessment of my fellowman by these same yardsticks constitutes what I see to be his or her identity. So, too, will be my assessment of events and of all that is going on around me. In every case, my assessments will be included in what I am accepting as mind, or mentality, and so in what

3

I am. It is not really personal, however much it appears to be that way, but is the universal picture of a material life parading as "my" heredity, "my" experience, circumstances, and so on. It is this that appears to determine the mud and stars of our experience.

Now, so long as this I, or ego, refers to a human mind — a particular version of the personal and physical framework of perception — experience will be seen to take on the character and nature of this mind. The mental lens through which everything is perceived or interpreted determines how we see it. We can find an analogy in a movie. The screen is clean and white, but the projections upon this screen may be good or bad, beautiful or ugly. These projections are inherent in the lens and do not belong to the screen. No amount of tampering with the screen can alter the phenomena projected upon it.

The Inadequacy of the Human Mind

The human mind, or lens, is an inadequate projector. Its nature is duality, and so everything seen through it polarizes as good and evil, life and death, hope and disappointment, and all the mingling of opposites that appears to make up human existence. But these pairs of opposites are not on the screen of experience. They are inherent in the human mind, or ego.

Another characteristic of existence seen through this lens — that is, of life as a mortal ego — is that awareness from this standpoint is always partial. St. Paul referred to this view of things as "Now I know in part"[1] and, of course, knowing in part, or as a particle of existence, presupposes two things. The first is that there will be many other parts, or particle egos, on which we are dependent, or to which we are related, which may or may not be thinking in the same way. Hence the scenario of wars, disputes, competition, distrust, and all the mental penury of daily existence. The good seems capricious, and a portion of good, a fair share, and a place in the sun, is the most that mortals can seem to hope for.

The second effect of "particle" awareness is that, although everything reaches one at the point of consciousness, the universe still appears to remain objective, solidly material, and so outside what we are knowing about it. Thus, any hope of exercising dominion over circumstances seems slight. The human substitute for this dominion is the attempt either to dominate or retreat from an external world. Thus arise the problems that have always faced religion and philosophy, namely, how to reconcile the mental, or spiritual, with the physical, or material. The unsatisfactory nature of particle experience is well summarized in a statement by the American physicist, Professor David Bohm, "We cannot, in the end, do anything but destroy if we have a fragmentary approach." This destruction is inevitable, because it reduces that which is essentially whole to bits.

The attempt to find an explanation for an apparently external universe from the standpoint of a human personality, or ego, must prove abortive. The human mind, which depends on the five physical senses, cannot be the means for reaching and discovering something higher than itself. The human personality — what we might term a "small i" perception— can no more transcend its own limitations than a fountain can rise higher than its source. But what if this human mind, so-called, is not really anything in itself, but just terminology for that which obscures and limits a higher selfhood and awareness?

Aldous Huxley, in his book, "The Doors of Perception," makes a remarkable assertion that each of us is really "Mind-at-large," and the word "Mind" is spelt with a capital "M." He continues by explaining that what appears as a personal, human mind is not something in its own right, but is simply a kind of filter mechanism that allows only that information to pass through which is of immediate application to personal experience. In other words, this so-called human mind is a term for limitation, and nothing else. It presents a false, limited view of things, whilst not making anything other than what it already is. It follows that, only by removing this filter mechanism, can the view be enhanced and the reality seen. This is what is meant by dealing with everything in and as consciousness. The lens, or mentality, is all-important. It should be noted, however, that Mind-at-large is no more touched by the limitation or filter than the sunlight is touched by the window pane through which it passes.

Evidence of Limitation

The human mind cannot transcend the limitations of its own nature. It will always be circumscribed by the tools on which it depends for information, namely, the five senses. We can see the evidence of this in three modes of thought, namely, science, theology, and medicine.

In each case, research is impelled by an assumption of some universal reality but suffers from the limitations of the five physical senses as vehicles of perception. The search for a new view is hampered by the lens at the viewpoint. No one would wish to deride the deep insights that have been obtained in these fields, nor ignore the devotion to God expressed by many of their finest thinkers. But, wherever truth breaks through, it has to be an ultimate reality appearing which is not wholly hidden by the opacity of an inadequate lens, and not the product of a human mind glimpsing it. Truth itself cannot be imprisoned within the limitations of a mortal "i" or ego.

In the research of the physical sciences, it is clear that there is no finality in the work. Each new discovery, far from offering a final answer, turns out to be a false crest — a basis from which a new assumption can be made. But there is always some unknown, some hypothesis, a "factor x," in this assumption without which the research cannot go forward. In short, however stupendous the goal, the basic tool for research remains the human mind. At no point can the lesser embrace the greater. Only by the fading out of a limited sense, or human mind, could that which is already included in Mind-at-large, or what we now might begin to call the universal, or divine, Mind, be apparent. This is why we have to deal with everything, not by trying to manipulate what is perceived through the human "mind" but by removing the lens.

In theology and religion the search is for ultimate Truth, or God, but the approach which assumes a little mortal trying to understand a big God has been found wanting. Because the tool for this attempt to understand Truth again remains the human mind, it cannot interpret correctly. God, or Truth, or that which IS, inevitably remains the great unknown, and the theological approach is increasingly rejected without too much appearing in its place to fill the vacuum. Prayer no longer seems to work, yet people want to feel and live by their beliefs, as witnessed by the growth of evangelized religion. This offers feeling as opposed to the intellectualizing of much mainline religion. Without the capacity to "feel" their faith, the essential ingredient is missing. Consequently, for all the glitz of material promises, existence for many remains hollow in the centre.

Third, in medicine, the attempt to change or improve phenomena must, to return to the analogy of the movie, be tantamount to concentrating on the screen, rather than the lens of the projector. Despite the work of dedicated men and women, the sum total of dis-ease in the world has not really lessened. Some problems are eliminated, but others appear. Indeed, some diseases which were thought to be eradicated, are reappearing, strengthened against the very medicines that were thought to have destroyed them. There is not a physical answer to apparently physical problems.

Even when the search is turned back to the mind, as it is increasingly, the focus is on mental disorder and psychosomatic diseases. It is still the human mind, with this mind's duality, that occupies attention. Its inherent ambivalence remains, and so ultimate healing tends to stay out of reach. It is a sign of the physical interpretation of everything yielding, but not more.

Needs Yield to Solutions

The failure of the human mind to rise above its limitations is seen now in the understandable and legitimate desire of so many people to find new methods to rise above their circumstances. This may appear in many forms. Meditation, self-realization, and other mainly Eastern techniques reflect the search for a higher self. The cult of personality, often in the most aggressive form but also in the many advertisements that offer ways to increase the effectiveness of the human personality, reflects the same desire to find and be something other than the thwarted and humdrum. A current magazine, for example, advertises books to "improve your self-image," "boost your belief in yourself," "act more effectively," "transform the way you talk to yourself," and "reclaim your inner happiness." The prevalence of drugs still points to the same desire for an enhanced experience, even though the method of achieving it is self-defeating and suicidal. In none of these cases, however, is the tool through which this betterment is expected to take place other than the human mind.

Yet the comfort behind all this is that, for all the frustration involved in any human approach to a final answer, the fact that people even seek such a thing implies an instinctive sense that it is actually present. It would be impossible to be aware of something, even though apparently remote, if it were not part of consciousness. As so often in history, the acute awareness of a need brings forth its solution. The initiative for discovery is always the fact that the truth already exists, and so is a necessity. It breaks through the mists of ignorance that, like the morning mist hiding the sun, cannot forever obscure it. Moreover, at no point in what appears as a process of enlightenment, is there ever a vacuum. The appearing of the sun is in exact ratio to the disappearance of the mist. The constantly clearer views of everlasting facts never leave a void in experience. While the frustration of the human search stems from the fact that the fountain cannot rise higher than its source or, more starkly, nothing cannot become something, the goal remains a possibility. The need to realize this possibility has never been greater, and its achievement becomes practical as we begin to ask, not *what* are we seeing, but *how* do we see? Then the search is along the right lines.

Interpretation from Principle

Perhaps the key to answering the question lies in a statement from Science of Health: "The divine Principle of the universe must interpret the universe."[2] Throughout history, the attempt has been made to interpret the universe from some standpoint outside the infinite — a standpoint of perception that is itself a contradiction in terms. We have already touched on the futility of such an attempt. But now this statement is saying that all correct interpretation has to be from the standpoint of Principle, or first cause, and not from effect or from the testimony of the physical senses.

The stupendous vision of Moses, for example, glimpsed the underlying essence of being in the recognition that the name, or nature, of God was I AM THAT I AM or, to paraphrase, perhaps one could say, "Truth is that which is." But Moses — a state of thought as much as a historical figure — did not entirely relinquish his belief that Truth somehow needed a human partner. He knew God, or Truth, to be a presence that would be with him and teach him what to say, but this very retention of a human sense of things that had to be accompanied and taught, kept a belief in duality. Thus, the Promised Land, which might be termed that spiritual state where, as Jesus put it, "I and my Father are one," was withheld from his experience. And it is still withheld from the Moses thought of today.

The teachings of Christ Jesus that man is one with God and that "the kingdom of God is within you"[3]— within the correct interpretation of being — were not understood by his followers. Indeed, he said that the time for this understanding could not come until the Spirit of Truth, rather than a personal Messiah, would teach all things.[4] The result was that the Christian churches have tended to follow in the footsteps of Moses, anticipating a Promised Land, or Kingdom of Heaven, that could be reached only after a desert march of forty years.

The Scientific Method of Proof

It is against this background that we can see the importance of interpreting the universe from the standpoint of its Principle, or first cause. In fact, this is the only way to understand any science. You start with its principle, and an understanding of this principle and the laws which express it shows up both what is true and what is not. By starting in any science with the premise, and staying with it, all that is true proves itself, whereas that which is not true disproves itself. This is important, if we are not to be swayed by the conflict between the testimony of the senses and the premise that we have decided is true. For example, we may say that God is Love. Then the physical testimony says, but children get hurt. So, do we abandon our premise, or do we let a new understanding of the principle of infinite Love reframe our perception of hurt children? In other words, do we stay with the principle and give it the same respect, or greater, that we have previously afforded its opposite, no matter what the physical evidence to the contrary may appear to be? To abide by the principle is important in any science, and how much more must this approach apply in the case of Divine, or Spiritual, Science, which defines the Principle, laws, and constituency of the entire universe in spiritual, instead of material, terms. This is a subject to which we shall return frequently in the course of this book. Divine Science is ✓ the Science of being: the understanding of what is already spiritually true and its accompanying practice. It is not the science of becoming, nor is it a philosophy without accompanying demonstration.

It is at this point that we can see the relevance of the first part of this chapter, which concentrated on the mind that we were accepting as our capacity to know. Consciousness is always in the present, and what might be termed either the Moses, or the Christian, or Principle's own standpoint of interpretation refers to present, not past, states of thought. The inherent limitation and duality of a human mind, so-called, is seen to be an inadequate tool, or lens, with which to perceive Truth. The implication of this is that its only usefulness lies in its fading out of the way. If this mind is just terminology for that which limits and obscures, then the less of it the better. It is not something that can understand more and more, but rather a term for ignorance that, in the presence of understanding, becomes less and less.This understanding constitutes the scientific I, or eye.

2

As "I" See It

If therefore thine eye be single, thy
whole body shall be full of light.

Christ Jesus

Whole, Not Partial, Knowing

The scientific "I," or eye, transcends the vision of the human lens and transforms all that is perceived through it. This is why, in reviewing the achievement and potential of science, theology, and medicine, the emphasis has been on the shortcomings of the human mind as the tool for perception, rather than any attempt to denigrate the standards and devotion with which the research has been conducted. It is because the human approach is inhibited by the senses through which information is gathered that the view obtained can be only partial. There has to be an ultimate, non-personal capacity to understand, if the truth is to be attained. This is why the term "spiritual" has to transcend the humanly mental. It has to refer to consciousness that emanates from the divine Mind — an infinite, indivisible, and universal consciousness that is not channeled through the medium of a human mind. As one writer has put it, " There is a force available to man which is superior to man's intellectual capacities."

Earlier, a part of a statement by St. Paul was quoted, namely, "Now I know in part." It continues, "but then shall I know even as also I am known." The implication of this is that partial, hence inaccurate, knowing has to yield to knowing that takes place from an unrestricted, and so

13

correct, standpoint. This standpoint of perception, or interpretation, has to be that of Principle, cause, and includes the recognition that the divine Mind, or God, is the only legitimate capacity to know. It is interesting that part of the oral culture of the Zulus in South Africa speaks of "the place where one goes to be known at last, as the first spirit has all along known one." As a limited lens is removed, the unobstructed, universal view is revealed. We can see a simple example of this in the light shining through the window pane. There is no inherent light in the pane, and to some degree the pane can only obscure the light. The clearest window pane allows the least obstructed view.

We have seen that mind, or mentality, affects experience. This is widely recognised. An insurance company, for example, accepts that certain types of character, reflected in the work that they do, are better risks than others. And we all know the difference of approach between those who hold a glass of water in their hand and say it is half-full, and those who see the same glass as half-empty. But this is only a step on the way to recognising that thinking does not just affect but actually constitutes experience, and this is because, to quote Sir Arthur Eddington, the former British Astronomer Royal, "to put the conclusion crudely, the stuff of this world is mind-stuff." We live in a world of consciousness, where the consciousness of something is that thing.

The New Standpoint

Two questions now present themselves. The first is, How do we let this Mind be our effective capacity to know? The second is, What is the result of knowing from the standpoint of the divine Principle of the universe?

In his letter to the Galatians, Paul spoke of the "fruit of the

Spirit," defining it as "love, joy, peace, longsuffering, gen-tleness, goodness, faith, meekness, temperance." And then he adds, "Against such there is no law."[1] Here we find a new level of consciousness. Instead of merely recognising the influence of human thinking on experience, Paul is speaking of a level of thought that is outside the material laws of cause and effect that make up human experience. The fruits of the Spirit are essentially the thoughts that emanate from the pure consciousness of the divine Mind. The divine Mind, or God, thinks these universal qualities of good. The awareness of the fruits of the Spirit is Mind's awareness of its own nature. This awareness is recognised to be not just desirable human qualities of thought but the actual consciousness of the divine Mind itself. As this awareness constitutes our thinking, experience is lifted outside the dream of material existence to the mental place where there is no contrary law. This is why we are talking about a science and not just a philosophy, for it involves both an understanding of that which *is* and car-rying it through into daily living.

This consciousness, transcending all the limitations imposed by the human lens, is yours and mine. When the thoughts or ideas of the divine Mind constitute aware-ness, then all there is to our thinking is Mind itself, not just affecting but actually constituting experience. That which is identified with the one I, or Ego, or Mind, has dropped all association with the little "i", or human per-sonality, and its restricted awareness. Knowing as this Mind, or Ego, means that consciousness and experience never deviate from the quality and character of its source, any more than the image in a mirror can deviate from rep-resenting the original in front of the mirror.

Before leaving this subject, let us put it to the test. We can ask, "How many times a day does one of these qualities, or fruits of the Spirit, actively engage our consciousness?

15

How many times do I just pause and contemplate the underlying harmony and inviolate nature of being?" If the answer is a poor one, then, "Why is my life what it is?" Our experience cannot reflect and express the fruits of the Spirit, if these fruits are not being cherished in and as consciousness. A friend was having a telephone conversation with a close relative who was letting fly with a barrage of criticism and abuse. Instead of taking this in and reacting, my friend just mentally spelt out the letters, "L.O.V.E." Nothing else was allowed to occupy her thought, and the whole situation resolved itself. In such detail is Principle practiced.

The Effect of the New Standpoint

Now we return briefly to the second question, namely, What is the result of knowing from this standpoint? To interpret from the standpoint of divine Principle instead of person or physical sense-testimony, allows us to see and experience the one and only universe as it really is, rather than as it appears to be. We have not altered what we see, but how we see it. The view is not changed, but the vision of it is enhanced. Mrs. Eddy once remarked, "I wish I could tell you what I see when I look into a rose." To live as a mortal in a material universe is simply to identify with the reports that the physical senses have made about their misconception of man as that little "i" or ego. To live as the eternal and perfect image of God is to live as that consciousness which consists solely of the thoughts of God, the fruits of the Spirit. This latter way of living was what enabled Christ Jesus, who appeared to those around him as a mortal like them, to say, " Ye are from beneath; I am from above."[2] His concern was the origin of his thinking, and this in turn proved that "against such there is no law," when the stones they threw at him found no target.

Hidden from the World

During World War II, an acquaintance found in his own experience that this same immunity was a law that applied today as in the time of Jesus. Consciousness that consists of the "fruits" of the Spirit is literally out of range and sight to another level of thought. He was Russian born and had escaped in a very wonderful way from his own country to France. It then became necessary for him to leave Paris, where he was living, and his proposed route would take him across the Pyrenees to Spain. Before he left, his mother, who had practiced this Science for many years, said to him, "Remember, you are invisible." By this she meant that the only I to know him, and the only eye to see him, was the divine Mind.

On reaching the foothills of the Pyrenees, he joined a small party who had a guide to take them across. They set out at dusk but were soon intercepted by an enemy patrol. Shots were fired, and the party was scattered. He found himself wandering alone on the mountainside. Then a thick mist came down, leaving a visibility of only a yard or so. During the night, he could hear sounds of the patrol. In the morning, there was a sudden clearing of the mist in a small area in front of him, and he saw there a shepherd boy who led him safely across the mountains into Spain. Later, he reached England, where he worked for the rest of the war with the BBC. For him, it was indeed proof of the verse from the psalm, "He that dwelleth in the secret place of the most High shall abide under the shadow of the Almighty."[3]

The Basis of Healing

Seeing with the scientific "I" is the key to healing. As Science and Health says, "Jesus beheld in Science [that is, with the Mind of God] the perfect man, who appeared to him [to that Mind] where sinning mortal man appears to mortals. In this perfect man the Saviour saw God's own likeness, and this correct view of man healed the sick."[4] It will be noted that it was the correct, and not the corrected, view that healed, for the divine Mind, or Principle, never knows anything to correct.

I recall visiting some children and being told their pony was lame. The vet had taken X-rays which showed an incurable fracture. He said that the pony must be put down, and that, as he was going away, his colleague would do what was needed. I went to the stable and said to the pony, "You have been listening to stable talk." I then explained to the children that the way this pony appeared to them was not the way that the Mind of God was seeing it. They understood that, in the very place that the human mind was seeing its upside down, incorrect view of things, the Mind that was God was seeing its own perfect expression — in terms of qualities, not outlined matter — and that was all that was true and present. It was not a matter of trying to visualise a perfect material horse, but realizing that just where the inversion presented a physical and sick picture was the presence of God in self-expression.

I then left for the Far East, and when I visited these friends again, some weeks later, they took me to see the pony, who was cantering round the field. Apparently, the vet had returned and asked why they had not called his colleague. They replied that they did not think it was necessary. The vet took a further set of X-rays, which showed a perfect healing of the foreleg. He said that this was outside his whole professional experience and sent the first and second set of photographs to the Royal College of Veterinary Surgeons.

The Nature of Subjectivity

A further aspect of this new and correct method of interpretation is that in it we find the true sense of subjectivity. Earlier, we have seen that the human interpretation of
apparently external events was subject, or subjective, to
the mind or "I" that was doing the interpreting. Now we
find that these events are not external at all, for everything
is reduced to thought, both in cause and effect. What is
termed the human mind presents a *sense* of being. We find
the *sense* of something is all there is to it, and that there is
no extension to consciousness. The first of these views
can be classified as misinterpretion, or mesmerism. The
second, or true, interpretation is reality.

A man went to India to learn something about mesmerism. He was met by his prospective teacher at the port
where he landed. It was a warm, calm day. Men were
unloading crates of cargo; small boats were at anchor in
the harbour. Suddenly, a violent storm blew up. Boats
were torn off their moorings; the cargo crates were hurled
into the sea, injuring the men who were unloading them.
There was chaos everywhere. Then the visitor saw the
teacher smiling, and he understood that he had been mesmerized. At once, the original scene was restored. No
boats were adrift, and the men carried on unloading, as if
nothing had happened. Indeed, this was the case.

Immunity from Riots

That which was true of the storm is equally true of the
crime and violence of today. Being is not phenomenal but
subject to the mentality or "I" that sees it. A few years
ago, Britain was torn by racial riots. Each night a different city was affected. One Saturday morning we were told
that the area where we lived was the target for that night.
Shopkeepers and home owners boarded up their windows
and waited.

Many others, however, prayed. They knew that the presence of God means the absence of everything unlike God, and that the only place this situation was to be handled was in consciousness, where the "correct view" was maintained. This attitude was neither mystic nor religious in a conventional sense, but practical living. You have problems where you do not have God. The general belief is that you have problems here, with God somewhere up there. This then means that you have one universe where you postulate God's presence, and another where you postulate His absence. And, in the terms we have been using, you either have the divine Mind present as consciousness, with the attendant fruits of the Spirit, or that Mind is absent, so far as you are concerned, and so you have the problems inherent in that absence. And this poses again the important question, How much of our thinking day consists of God or good with us? If it is a good part of the day, do we find that good not with us diminishes as our experience? This, of course, is the test. So try it! As Laura Huxley put it, "It works if you work it."

In the case of the impending riot, nothing happened. Moreover, that was the end of these riots in Britain. But there was a sequel — a necessary one to complete the story. My wife was working at the time with a gilder in South London to whom she was apprenticed. On the Monday following, he said to her, "You know, an extraordinary thing happened on Saturday. As it was getting dusk, I watched about eight hundred youths assembling and getting ready to cross the river to where you live and make trouble. Suddenly, without any coercion at all, they began to break up and disperse. The police were doing nothing. There was nothing to stop them from carrying out their intentions. Now, what do you make of that?" We thought we knew what to make of it. Many people pray at a time of crisis. Why should they be surprised if their prayers are answered, or attribute the answer to anything but prayer?

We find that thoughts are things, and that the thought, or sense, of something is its substance, its underlying essence. A thought requires a mind to think it, and the substance, or consciousness, of a thought resides, not in the thought, but in the mind that thinks it. The thoughts of the divine Mind remain in Mind and partake of the nature and character of that Mind. In the degree that consciousness consists of the thoughts of God, the fruits of the Spirit, they constitute our nature and experience. When these thoughts, the actual presence of God, are our consciousness, the thoughts which postulate the absence of God, or good, are not present. This is why the prophet, Isaiah, defined the Saviour as "Immanuel, or God with us,"[5] for when God, good, is with us as our thinking and living, it saves us from the mesmerism of belief that God, good, is not with us. This is the Saviour consciousness, against which there is no law, and the capacity to know Truth from the standpoint of Truth is the Christ. This Christ saves effectually, while knowing nothing to save.

We will return to many of these themes later in this book, but it may be helpful to summarize some basic points from these opening chapters.

Summary

1. Consciousness is fundamental. We live in a universe of thought, not matter, and this is something that is also being discovered by modern physics.

2. Thoughts require a mind to think them. The thoughts of a so-called human mind do not have any inherent reality but are the misconceptions of the ideas that are always

21

present and substantial to the divine Mind or God, the one I or Ego.

3. The only standpoint from which the universe can be correctly interpreted is that of its Principle, or cause. Only thus does the unknown God become knowable, since the divine Mind, or Principle, affords the only capacity to know. It becomes our capacity as our thought is found in relation to the divine by expressing the qualities of the divine.

4. Only in finding a higher nature and selfhood derived from God, and in relinquishing any identity with anything less, can the otherwise abortive attempt of the human personality to transcend its inherent limitations be realized.

5. It is the correct view or interpretation, that is, from universal — not localized — consciousness that heals, comforts, redeems, and saves.

The essence of this Divine Science is to think, or know, wholly instead of humanly or partially. This occurs as a result of unconditional identity with and as the universal Mind, the pure altitude of awareness that is conscious of its own eternal, flawless, unopposed sense of being. This understanding of true identity is not intellectual, but is the inevitable entitlement that accompanies growth in Christian character, the character of the Christ, as exemplified by the Master.

We learn to know as Mind, and not as a person knowing about Mind. It means living in the detail of daily experience as the divine Life, and not just as a person trying to live a good life.

What does this mean in practice? Let us look at an example. Someone cuts in on you when you are driving a car.

And, clearly, dealing with other people seems to comprise a great deal of life. So what is your reaction? To try to regain your position with appropriate language? That is obviously not the best way. A humanly good person will restrain his or her desire to hit back. But the consciousness of the divine Life is unaware of interference, for it knows nothing to interfere with itself. Knowing our oneness with this Life means that any apparent forebearance is a matter of grace rather than human self-control.

True living entails awareness as Truth, conscious of itself as all there is, and not just being a seeker after Truth. To be God-like, or good-like, means knowing and living from the standpoint of Principle, not person, for in the divine Mind no sense of a personal, limited approach is known. The way is increasing release from the personal point of view, which consists only of the impressions gained through the physical senses, and so is just a finite sense of the infinite. This is what it means to "put off the old man," the old viewpoint, by ceasing to identify with him, and to put on the new who "is renewed in knowledge after the image of him that created him."[6] From a human viewpoint this might seem arduous; from a divine, it is just the falling away of the trivial and second-rate without struggle. It is the viewpoint, or lens, that determines the view, and it is in looking out through the lens of the divine Mind that everything appears as I, the scientific I or Ego, see it. The single eye, quoted at the head of this chapter, is the eye or "I" that constitutes the correct lens with which we view. The result of this viewpoint is that the whole body, the whole of our experience, is characterized by it, and the view is transformed.

3

The Order of Science

The Son can do nothing of himself, but what
he seeth the Father do: for what things soever
he doeth, these also doeth the Son likewise.
Christ Jesus

"Particle" Existence Obsolete

We have seen that, so long as we identify ourselves as a bit of existence called a mortal, our universe is going to appear external to what we call ourself, and consisting of other bits, each in its own orbit, each doing its own thing — something we may, or may not, find congenial. Moreover, the very assumption of a "particle" existence means that we regard this mortal as having a capacity to act, see, hear, know, and so on. The inevitable result of this assumption, as human history has shown, is chaos.

In this context, a significant statement in Science and Health summarizes the scientific order in which true being can be understood: "In the order of Science, in which the Principle is above what it reflects, all is one grand concord. Change this statement, suppose Mind to be governed by matter or Soul in body, and you lose the keynote of being, and there is continual discord."[1]

The Keynote of Being

This "keynote of being" rests on the fact that the Principle is above what it reflects. The relationship of man to God is subsidiary. We can see examples of this fact in everyday life. An obvious one is that of the reflection in the mirror. Clearly, this reflection has no life, substance, or

24

capacity of its own, for it is simply the reflex image of that which is taking place in front of the mirror. Indeed, if that which is in front of the mirror moves away, there is no reflection left. It must also be clear that reflection has no capacity to be aware of itself, neither can it be aware of its original. If it could, then reflection would embrace the original, which is impossible.

Using the word "reflection" in a rather different way, we can use another analogy. If you decide on some action, you probably first think it through. You look at its possibilities; you ponder; you reflect upon it. In this case, reflection is the mental activity in which you are engaged. The same conclusions follow, namely, that the idea you have does not, in turn, generate another idea, neither can your idea think about you. Otherwise it would be greater than you. You embrace the idea in your mind.

Expression but Not Expressors

In any science, the ideas, rules, or laws that constitute the body of that science exist in their principle. They express that principle but are not expressors. They reflect it but are not reflectors. The same is true in Spiritual Science. The ideas that express the divine Principle, and which constitute the body or manifestation of that Principle, have no life or capacity of their own. Man is reflection, image. He initiates nothing. He is the evidence to his Principle of what that Principle is. This is why the consciousness of an idea is not in the idea but in the Mind that has the idea.

Now, in the understanding that the whole of our experience takes place in the Principle in front of the mirror, the inevitable harmony results from the fact that one Principle, or Mind, means one thinker, one source of action, supply, feeling, knowing. This necessarily pre-empts the discord of many minds, many thinkers, disagreements, portions, competition, and so on. One Principle does not misunderstand itself. It does not disagree with or make war on itself. It does not allocate portions of itself, nor does it compete with itself, since allness is its measure, and portions do not enter its premise or conclusion. "The sun sends forth light, but not suns; so God reflects Himself, or Mind, but does not subdivide Mind, or good, into minds, good and evil."[2]

Does it not follow that the apparent discord in the world is not primarily because of what many minds, or so-called actors and reflectors, are doing, but because the keynote of being has been misinterpreted? To believe that Mind is in matter makes matter more than Mind. To think that Soul is in body, is to make Soul subsidiary to body. To work on the assumption that Principle is in idea is to lose the Principle. None of this would be the way for intelligent Mind to run the universe, and the attempt to reason back from effect to cause, and explain the discord by saying it is the effect of man's exercising free will, would mean that evil was coexistent and co-eternal with God. And, in this case, how could this consciousness of evil be also the means of redemption from it?

Ignorance and Understanding

The keynote of being is lost only in belief, for its harmony abides with its Principle and so is inseparable from it. Hence, the statement that "It is our ignorance of God, the divine Principle, which produces apparent discord, and the right understanding of Him restores harmony."[3] The right understanding of cause necessarily includes an understanding of the relationship of effect to cause, or man to his Principle. In fact, it is impossible to understand man except from the standpoint of his Principle, since only that which stands, so to speak, in front of the mirror can see the image. But, in adopting this new and correct interpretation of everything from and as the Mind that is Principle, we see the harmony and grand concord of being as it always is and has been — a view that a false viewpoint may seem to hide but can never touch.

A lady who had recently been widowed opened a shop and started her new work by selling the antiques and pictures from her home. She was a devout Anglican, and her faith was a great support in this difficult time. One day she had her first exhibition of pictures. I called on her in the morning on my way to work, as I was unable to attend the opening. She told me that she was in such pain from her legs that she did not see how she was going to get through the day. I said to her, " You have never stood on your own feet." Her reply was, "Of course," and we said good-bye. That evening she telephoned to say she had been on her feet all day, going up and down three flights of stairs, without a vestige of pain. She went on to become one of the more successful art dealers in London. The order of Science did not include a separate entity that had to stand alone, separate from its Principle.

Principle in Practice

The important question, of course, is how to make this practical. As always, the answer is, begin with God, or Principle. This entails three steps. The first is to know and apprehend more of the divine nature. Only as we understand and embody the true nature of Life, of Truth, of Love, and the other aspects of God, can we find a yardstick by which to measure what man is, and thus also what he is not. The command to "know thyself" is possible to fulfill only by first knowing God, and then knowing from the standpoint of God. It is from this standpoint that the true self can be seen, for Mind knowing itself is yourself.

The second stage is listening. In effect, it means asking

oneself all the time, "What is true of this situation from the standpoint of God rather than from that of the physical senses?" This is why a knowledge of God is the first prerequisite, because only that knowledge can convey an understanding of what God is being at any moment. To Jesus, it was the understanding of Truth that freed from sickness. It was the consciousness of Life that was more real than the evidence of death. And it was the awareness of Love that protected from and precluded the onslaughts of hate.

The third stage follows naturally. It is the renunciation of human will, planning, speculating, judging, or condemning. Only through self-abnegation, the abandonment of all identity with a self that is less than, or separate from, God can the voice and direction of Principle be heard. This does not mean making our own arrangements, and then asking God to bless them. It means letting thought and action be captive to Principle, irrespective of what the senses are suggesting. God, not man, does God's will, for Principle is self-enforcing.

And why should we not do this? The evidence of man's attempt to steer the boat would suggest that a change of captain is desirable. In the loss of a human sense of capacity, our daily life is not depleted but enhanced. As the mist of ignorance that would hide what Principle is already doing is dissolved, it appears as greater wisdom, perspicacity, and intelligence; it appears as more lively, lovely, caring, feeling people; it appears as joy emancipated from sorrow, activity emancipated from burden, abundance emancipated from want. The reason is that the one Life is shining with greater clarity through the mists of corporeality. Mortal man has nothing to lose but his chains.

Man is the experience of good but not the experiencer, for the capacity to experience remains in the Principle. Man is the reflection of all that resides in his divine origin but is not a reflector. Man is the song but not the singer; the music but not the musician; the painting but not the artist. And yet they are one, for neither could be without the other. It is the artist, the musician, the Principle that, in every case, maintains its harmony.

A lady who had been caring for an elderly relative was suffering from arthritis. Her wrists and ankles were swollen; she had been unable to wear ordinary shoes for two years, and she had other physical problems. A practitioner called on her, and she said to him: "What is my sin? I am pure in thought and deed, yet look at the state I am in." He replied, "No one could be humanly more pure than you, but the mistake lies in believing that the responsibility for this situation rests on you. In that this represents the failure to recognise that God alone does the work of God, it is a sin." Immediately, she replied, "Of course, I see the mistake." On the following morning she called to say that her wrists were normal, she was wearing shoes, and free from pain. The whole situation with her relative resolved itself in a day or so. In fact, more prayer was needed later before she was fully free, but the immediate result showed the mental nature of the problem, and it also showed that freedom was incidental to an altitude of consciousness rather than a change in physical circumstances.

The relinquishment of a false sense of ego — all that constitutes the history and circumstances of a personal "i"— may seem hard, but only until we understand, either through intelligence or through sharp experience, that in fact there never was a true identity outside the one I, or Principle. Then it is the concord, instead of the discord, that I am experiencing.

4

Appearance and Reality

*Blessed are the eyes that are shut off from external
things and are fixed upon the things within.*
                                        Thomas à Kempis

The attempt to reconcile Spirit and matter has never borne
fruit. Their substance and origin are diametrically
opposed. Nevertheless, the tendency has been to admit
both as valid and, in some way, connected. Jewish and
Christian theology have taught that man has a soul
derived from God, but also a "vile body," made of the dust
of the ground. At some point, the first departs from God,
and the second reverts to its native dust. Eastern philosophy terms the objective world of the material senses "illusion" but tends to see the material and physical as a valid
stage on the way to a higher level of existence. In both
West and East there is an admitted interdependence, if
only for a period, between matter and mind.

Beyond Materialism

Christian Science defines matter in a number of ways that
indicate its mental nature but also continues up to the
explanation that, here and now, all that actually exists is
the divine Mind and its ideas. Some of the terms used in
Science and Health to define matter include "theoretical
mind," "the substratum of mortal mind," "illusion," "that
of which immortal Mind takes no cognizance," "that
which mortal mind sees, feels, hears, tastes, and smells
only in belief," and "an error of statement."[1] Matter, in
these definitions, is not just redefined mentally; the so-
called mind that it expresses is theory and so is something
which might be called educational terminology, but no more.

Again, in Science and Health, we read that "the categories of metaphysics rest on one basis, the divine Mind. Metaphysics resolves things into thoughts, and exchanges the objects of sense for the ideas of Soul."[2] This process does not stop at recognising that what appears to the physical senses as material, externalised things and objects of sense is really just a set of mental impressions. It continues up to the recognition that Soul, the only Ego or Mind, alone conceives, and so what appears at one level as impressions of the human mind exists essentially as ideas of the divine Mind. The reality is the idea of this Mind, and the impression of the human mind is its restricted sense and inversion. From this we can see that the "half-way house" of a mentalized universe, which is still subject to the duality of the human mind, yields to the Science of being in which the one, infinite Mind has no opposite.

Analogies can be useful. For example, the apparently bent stick, reflected in the water, is a mental impression, since we know that the stick is not bent at all. It is apparent only to the mental standpoint that is looking at the distorted image rather than the straight original. But if the straight original is all that is occupying our attention, then there is no occasion to be looking at the image and no standpoint from which this is being done. Neither the distortion, nor the mental standpoint to which it is apparent, is of consequence. Similarly, the apparent movement of our train at a station, when it is really the train alongside which is moving, is a false impression; as, too, is the apparent convergence of the railway lines in the distance. Galileo proved that the impression of the solar system revolving around the earth was a false one, maintained only by the material organization that fostered belief in it. The physical sense of the universe is not reliable.

It is clear that any attempt to explain what the physical

senses see by means of these same senses merely com-
pounds problems. This is why, as always, the requirement
is to let the divine Principle of the universe interpret the
universe. In other words, we reason from the standpoint
of that Principle, or Mind, accepting as our only yardstick
that which is true from this standpoint, no matter how
such reasoning refutes the time-honoured conclusions
drawn from the testimony of the physical senses. To reason otherwise would be to accept the built-in contradictions of those senses. As we adopt this new reasoning, two
results became apparent.

The first is that all sense of duality begins to dissolve. We
are no longer starting with a human mind and then trying
to enhance the good while ridding ourselves of the bad it
seems to contain. We see that the material sense of things
is itself ruled out, because it cannot enter into the premise
or conclusion of thought which proceeds from the divine
Mind. Our sole concern now is with what we are accepting as Mind, knowing that the culprit behind all woes, as
well as the basis of every belief in a material existence, is
the human mind and is not to be found in its phenomena.
As we saw in Chapter 1, the phenomena of a false sense
are included in that sense.

Subjective Dominion

The second result is that we understand more clearly the
subjective nature of everything. All that appears to the
human mind as objects of sense and things external to
consciousness, is now found to be forms of thought inherent in the Mind that thinks them. It is only in this way that
we comprehend the dominion that was originally bestowed
upon man, and which the inverted sense of the human
mind misinterprets as the attempt to exercise domination
over others and an external environment. It is, in fact, possible to have dominion only over one's own thinking;

nothing else. But, when our starting point is one, infinite, wholly good Mind, then the universe of that Mind is not only subject to the Mind that conceives it but partakes of its nature and character as Love.

In reality, everything is the divine Mind in self-expression as qualities and not as objects of sense. The variety and beauty of the landscape, the grace and symmetry of a tree, the colours of a herbaceous border, the tenderness with which an animal cares for its young, the scintillation of a river in the sunlight, all point back to Mind. And the more everything is seen in this way, the more our experience of everything comes under the protection of this Mind, and shows forth the qualities of the divine, instead of a limited human sense of Life. Even the flowers in your vase will last longer when their reality and substance are seen to be the spiritual which cannot be wholly hidden by the belief they are material. The belief in a material mind that can think and outline, together with its limited phenomena, yields to the divine Mind and the eternal ideas that express it. The reality is never in the material appearance.

The Inverted Sense

We thus distinguish between the forms of mortal mind, or illusion, and those of the divine Mind, which are substance. We do not accord equal validity to both but recognise that the former are but inversions of that which is true here and now, with no more substance than a mirage. The former are beliefs, because they do not satisfy the criteria of true ideas, which are universal and eternal. They yield to the divine Mind. But the two do not comprehend or touch each other any more than the belief that 2+2=5 has any connection with the true idea that it is 4. Beliefs and ideas are not known to each other. The material universe is an upside down view of the spiritual but does not occupy space, have substance, or offer an alternative any more than does a mirage. This assessment is described helpfully in the passage from Science and Health, "Delusion, sin, disease, and death arise from the false testimony of material sense, which, from a supposed standpoint outside the focal distance of infinite Spirit, presents an inverted image of Mind and substance with everything turned upside down."[3]

An upside down image is never an alternative to the true but *is* the true seen wrongly. In the above quotation, it is still Mind and substance that are presented. A trained photographer can look at a negative and read the positive picture of which it is the reverse. A trained metaphysician, regarding everything from the standpoint of the divine Mind, can see the ideas of Soul in place of the objects of sense or the thoughts of the human mind. "Through faith [spiritual understanding] we understand that the worlds were framed by the word of God, so that things which are seen were not made of things which do appear."[4]

We can be specific. Lack, disease, unemployment, friction, wars are not objective states to be put right by trying to do something to the phenomena. They are impressions of a limited mind, real only to itself. They are to be dissolved in the understanding of what is already present and unlimited to the divine Mind. They are impressions that belong and are real to the three-dimensional world of material sense and fade in the wider scope of the spiritual dimension. Thus, the change takes place in thought, not in the phenomena. In no other way can the ills of mankind be healed. The viewpoint determines the view.

Here is an example which indicates a new approach. A friend had attended a talk on the subjective nature of being as well as its underlying perfection. The following morning, a Sunday, he was wakened by his children quarrelling in the next room. Normally, he said, he would have

34

gone in to read the riot act! This time, remembering what he had been discovering, he remained where he was, and just knew that the one Mind contained only thoughts of peace and love. Thus, any other thought-impressions were invalid. Immediately the noise next door ceased, and he had learned something of the right way of dealing with it. He gained a true sense of dominion, which had escaped him so long as he had resorted to "interpersonal" power tactics. An early teacher of Christian Science, when being told of someone's hearing a baby cry, remarked, "That which heard the baby cry made the baby cry." All aspects of the occurrences of a dream remain within the dream or illusion.

Another example, perhaps on a bigger scale, but still demonstrating the same rule, took place when I was returning with a party of students from a skiing holiday. The crossing of the English Channel from Ostend to Dover took about four hours and, on this occasion, the seas were so rough that there was doubt about our leaving port. When we eventually did so, the seas appeared mountainous. Almost at once people on deck began to be sick and went below. I said to one member of the party, who was familiar with Christian Science, "This sea is a mental, not a physical, impression, and the only Mind that can form a mental impression is the Mind that is God, and it sees peace, not turbulence." Very soon after, another man, who had no metaphysical background, came up and said "Do you see what I see?" It appeared that while the seas around were as rough as ever, we were sailing through a trough of almost calm water. As we watched, people who had gone below deck reappeared and began to laugh and play ball games. We continued our smooth passage until we reached Dover.

There was nothing miraculous about this; rather was it the demonstration of a law that we either do not always know, or we forget. It might be asked whether, below deck, there were others who were still being sick. Perhaps there were. What was important was that everything within the orbit of our consciousness was seen in a new light.

Harmonious Being

Everything that is true exists, but its substance is consciousness, not matter, and its location is within the divine Mind. "All that really exists is the divine Mind and its idea, and in this Mind the entire being is found harmonious and eternal."[5] Everything that appears to be an object of sense — and so subject to the duality and character of the human mind — is, when seen correctly, some idea or aspect of the divine Mind and so partakes of the nature of that Mind. A tree, a sunset, a home, a job, what have you, exist as some form of Mind. Down to the smallest detail, the universe of Mind, where we dwell, is showing forth the substance, nature, and perfection of that Mind here and now.

It is, of course, true that the mental nature of everything has been recognised by many people, not least by hypnotists, who can make their subjects see and do what they are mentally imposing upon them. All of us must have had some experience of this. But these displays are confined to the phenomena of the human mind, exchanging one concept for another. At this level, therefore, the misuse of such power is as likely as its use for apparent good. In either case, no one is really benefited by yielding his or her mentality to another, nor is the basic point recognised, namely, that the whole dream of material existence is the imposition of the material lens, and thus remains but an inversion of what is fundamentally true. True Mind-power cannot be misused, for its operation lies beyond and above the illusion of many minds in the wholeness of universal being.

Mind's Immediacy

The ideas of the divine Mind, on the other hand, are wholly good. The power of this Mind cannot be misused, since it is seen to operate only as the supposed power and influence of any other mind yield to its presence. The divine Mind is not engaged in producing rabbits out of a hat, or castles in the air, even though such feats seem common to those who operate at a mental, rather than spiritual, level. But, such is the omnipotence of the divine Mind that every idea that it contains is immediately — that is, without medium — tangible and appears in the highest appreciable form in human experience. In losing the misconception you have a higher sense of what is. But you lose nothing, because there is only one universe, and so there is no vacuum.

The idea of abundance or activity might well appear as income and work; the idea of completeness might well be appreciable as marriage or friendship. But such happy and inevitable results do not stem from any attempt to change the world of appearances or to outline how the truth might appear. Such an explanation would only involve exchanging one human belief for another. It is the melting of the ignorant world of appearances that allows what is already present to emerge more clearly, just as the sunlight, which is never absent, emerges through the morning mist. Mrs. Eddy once said, "If you do not let the outward become the inward, then the inward will take care of the outward."

The Lesson of the Picnic

Here is an illustration to show the difference between the inward and the outward. The picnic I had by the water in the Scottish Highlands is the picnic I had on the top of Table Mountain in South Africa, as well the one I enjoyed in an olive grove in Italy. Why? Because the substance of each occasion was the idea, the thought, of it. The beauty, relaxation, company, and satisfaction that were present were all constituent aspects of my own being, never outside consciousness, and so unchanging. The idea of these occasions remained in Mind, and so was and is as present as that Mind. The belief about them, of course, professed to be external to consciousness, in matter. The acceptance of the belief, instead of the idea, would mean that, no matter how enjoyable the occasions might appear to be, they would be limited to person, place, or thing. Personal company would be fleeting. To locate the picnic in some material place would be to confine it, and render it liable to the duality of experience that is the character of everything seen through the material lens. To hold it as an event in time would be to relegate it to the past. Then all that would remain would be either a memory or an expectation that one day something similar might repeat itself. The substance of the picnic would therefore elude me, and the thieves of person, place, and thing would have stolen its reality.

To externalise any good is to divide, and so to compare, and so to criticise and judge, and so to cease to love, and so to lose it. To externalise experience is also to place it in the time world where the relentless sequence of events leaves an irredeemable past in the wake of a dissolving present that awaits a future that remains out of reach. The comment of the tentmaker in the Rubaiyat of Omar Khayyam is all too relevant:

> The Moving Finger writes; and having writ,
> Moves on: Nor all thy piety nor wit
> shall lure it back to cancel half a line
> Nor all Tears wash out a word of it.

Only as everything is recognized to exist as idea, or conciousness, does it cease to be sequential and is it found to belong to the eternal here and now.

Christ Jesus warned that, if a house, or consciousness, were to stand, it must be built on a rock. To build on sand would be to invite its destruction by wind and rain or other external forces. Behind the metaphor is the profound fact that, unless the consciousness of something proceeds from and remains in the divine Mind, instead of from the testimony of the physical senses, it can be only ephemeral and vulnerable. It could have no firm foundation but would remain elusive like the fool's gold at the rainbow's end. Whatever belief fabricates, belief can take away. This is because the reality and substance of everything we experience are in the idea of it, and not the illustration. Picnics may change their character and venue, but the idea alone remains.

In a universe of consciousness, everything is thought. The highest concept of the human mind is but the illustration, the inverted view, of that which exists and stays in the divine Mind as idea. The sense of something is all there is to that thing. To themselves the five physical senses do not just affect experience; they constitute it. In the same way, the divine sense of being *is* the truth, or idea, of everything. Nothing takes place outside of thought. The physical sense of anything may inform you that there is something, but it can never be the substance. In other words, it can tell you that there is such a thing as a picnic, just as a mirage can inform you that there are trees and water, but the substance, form, and reality of them are not where they appear to be. The mirage remains the inverted view of some truth. Externalization is "shadow-thinking." That which proceeds from the divine Mind is "substance-thinking."

The health that I see in another is really the wholeness of

my own being. The home that I had yesterday, and exchanged for the one I have today, and will be the one that I will have tomorrow is the one, unchallenged, unchanging idea that I forever include. It is not in the illustration or temporary form of appearance. Likewise, the good that I expect is already my present consciousness, and the opportunities I thought I had missed yesterday have never left the divine Mind and so are present today. We live in this universe of ideas, and these are ever-present and constitute all substance. They will come forth in the highest appreciable form at any time, but the important thing is to recognise that the appearing as illustration is never the substance. In this way, we can enjoy whatever appears at the moment, without the bane that would attach itself to the same experience seen through the lens of the physical senses. There will never be a vacuum, because Mind cannot be without the idea of itself. But the inversion yields to the substance; the ephemeral to the eternal; the appearance to the underlying reality; and the myth to the reality. Then we find satisfaction in the true idea rather than in its illustration, knowing that whatever the external appearance, it can never deplete, augment, confirm, or deny the omnipresence of the divine Mind and its perfect idea that represents it and that constitutes what I AM.

The Inward and the Outward.

In reality, there is not an inward *and* an outward. The concept that, in some way, it is possible to transfer something from the inward to the outward, so that some inward idea can be repeated in some outward phenomenon, makes little sense. The infinite is one, not two. Nothing really exists in the "outward." The belief that it does has resulted in the endless attempt to change phenomena for the better, and this simply has not worked. Rather the opposite. It is only within consciousness that the ideas of the divine Mind are separated from the beliefs of human ignorance. It is not possible to manipulate the dream.

This does not mean neglect of human duty, but it does ensure its more effective discharge. Living out from the divine sense of things, the duties of the human realm appear less arduous and are carried out more by grace than effort. Our sense of duties changes. The feeling of being trapped in an endless round of demands that are imposed from outside yields, as man is found to be the activity of the divine Mind but not an independent actor. In fact, duties are never the problem in themselves. It is the material sense of them that makes any burden, and this sense disappears before the conscious presence of divine, effortless Life.

The importance of understanding where substance is truly to be found is apparent in a world where the frail and pre-carious nature of what has been thought to be substance is exposed. The belief in the external is crumbling. Substance in matter leads to competition and disappointment. Spiritual ideas do not. Spiritual ideas cannot be gained or lost except by choice, for while we may involuntarily lose our material possessions, we cannot be involuntarily stripped of our spiritual heritage. Spiritual substance, or Truth, belongs to all. It can be used freely yet never used up, any more than we can exhaust the supply of numbers and notes. The assurance is that, in dropping the exter-nalised view of substance and reality — the world of appearance — nothing that is substantial and real can be lost. Lost they cannot be, but in their restoration to where they belong, they are found to be as safe, permanent, and tangible as the eternal Mind itself, to which they are always known.

5

The Breakup of Materialism

*And this word, Yet once more, signifieth the
removing of those things that are shaken, as of
things that are made, that those things which
cannot be shaken may remain.*
                                        Hebrews

*The world begins to look more like a great
thought than a great machine.*
                                 Sir James Jeans

When we look at something from the standpoint of the
scientific "I," our concern is with its appearance at the
point of consciousness rather than its phenomena. As this
happens, the material *sense* of what is happening yields to
a spiritual sense. The substance of what we experience is
recognised as an idea in Mind instead of an object of
sense, and so it is found having the character of that Mind
instead of expressing the nature of the human lens.

This new viewpoint may be stated first as a shift in religious concepts, but like anything true, it is appreciable at
many levels. The disenchantment with a material view of
things is accompanied by the explanations of modern
physics that matter is not what it seems to be as well as by
changes of thought at all levels.

This is, in fact, a pattern that can be discerned in history.
It appears as a relationship between new religious concepts and what might be called their spin-off, first in the
physical sciences, and second in social behaviour, the

arts, and human experience and standards in general. At each stage we find matter being redefined.

Newtonian Mechanisms

For example, the established order at the time of the Holy Roman Empire, in which everyone had his or her allotted role to play, was challenged by the advent of Protestantism. The development of a secularized religion was supported by Newtonian physics, which portrayed the universe as a divinely ordained machine. The revised goals and mores of the population, even though they might lead in the ways of Mammon, reflected a new emancipation of thought. The divide between soul and body, and between spiritual and material experience, became greater in Europe than anywhere else in the world. The spread of a materialist view of everything reached its zenith at the turn of the nineteenth century. Darwin saw man as the product of a mechanical, evolutionary process; Marx saw the economy as a self-regulating mechanism; and Freud, though opening the door on psychology, saw even the human personality, with its id, ego, and super-ego, in terms of the gear-wheels of the mind. Two shattering world wars marked the ending of this era of thought.

A New Impetus in Thought

Already a new impetus was being felt in the discovery of a Christian, or spiritual, Science. The recognition of a metaphysical interpretation of existence which, by that time, had reached a critical mass, was beginning to be accepted as the only one which would prove truly valid. The fallout of this discovery then appeared, in turn, in two ways. First, was its counterpart appearing as mental science, and an interest in the potential use of the human mind. Theosophy, for example, appeared exactly at this moment. Second, the inversion of the scientific order, in which the Principle is above what it reflects, was seen in the upsurge of human dictators and "leaders" bent on war and claiming to usurp divine authority.

At the same time, the physical sciences were again challenging established theories. Relativity began to push out Newtonian physics, and a philosophy of relative values, in which "anything goes," began to overturn the standards of established acceptance in politics, social behaviour, dress, and the arts. "Thought, loosened from a material basis but not yet instructed by Science, may become wild with freedom and so be self-contradictory."[1] This period of becoming wild with freedom could be only an interim one. The fundamental change of framework which loosens belief in a material basis, either for the worship of God or the conduct of daily life, has brought about a new physics and, it can be postulated, an emergence of new standards as thought is instructed by Science. In physics, we find such statements as that of Professor David Bohm, "My view is to say 'I am the noumenon. At least I am of the noumenon. I am participating in the noumenon.' " The interpretation of the universe from the standpoint of its causative Principle, whereby thought looks out from instead of up to Mind, is emerging.

A New and Spiritual Basis

Divine Science states that being is one infinite, indivisible whole which consists, not of a number of cooperating parts, but of an infinite coordination of ideas. These emanate from the one Mind and are amenable to their Principle alone. Not surprisingly, physics echoes this statement in finding that beneath the apparently random behaviour of particles, governed by no higher law than probability, is a deep and underlying harmony. One physicist, Dr. Andrews of Johns Hopkins University, has described this as " the music of the spheres." And, in society as a whole, there is a discernible move away from random and lawless behaviour to some recognition that old standards have, after all, merit. A new and intelligent morality is appearing. At this period all traditional definitions of matter cease to apply.

Uncomfortable Transitions

The transition between an old and new order, which is taking place today, is neither even nor comfortable. It is uneven because progress in some areas seems almost offset by reversions to lawlessness in others. It is necessary to watch the underlying graph of growing spirituality rather than the fluctuation of surface phenomena. The transition is also uncomfortable, anyhow for those who hold to a receding past yet cannot capture the unfolding possibilities for the future. They are more concerned with what is disappearing than with the excitement of new vistas and the underlying reality behind them.

We can therefore usefully remember the verse quoted at the beginning of this chapter. The point to remember is that no matter what shaking appears to be taking place across the spectrum of human experience, we do not have to be shaken with it. It is only the human view that is being removed. The passing of an old order happens only because a higher and more satisfactory order awaits. The blossom shines through the bud. A wrong view never made a wrong fact, and the underlying order of Science is never shaken.

No Vacuums

It is at this point that we can remind ourselves of three points. The first is that the disappearance of a false sense does not involve the loss of a single thing that is real. All that is removed is a finite sense of the infinite. But the infinite remains. The disappearance of the mist before the morning lights enhances, but does not deplete, the landscape, which stays what it always is.

The second is that this disappearance is a factor of the appearance or self-assertion of Truth, and implies no capacity, in the human sense, either to retain or discard its inherent ignorance. The dawn is associated with many wonderful phenomena — the opening of the flower, the morning chorus of birds, the expectations of a new day — but all these are incidental to the emergence of the light.

The third point, which follows, is that our concern is only with the Science of being — the eternal Truth — and not with the states and stages of any human appearing. These stages simply reflect a diminishing sense of all that would obscure what is true, but are nothing in their own right.

A Disenchantment with Materialism

The growing recognition that what we term matter is but a misnomer, and that consequently matter is not the substance we have been educated to think it is, turns thought into new and spiritual channels. This new recognition of what is true and substantial has two results. The first appears as the breakup of materialism: that is, a disintegration of a material and objective explanation of everything. The second is a growing disenchantment with what a material world and the technology that accompanies it are offering. An appreciation of what science and technology can do *for* us is being replaced by a concern for what it is doing *to* us.

The above statements do not mean that everyone everywhere has accepted them. It would appear that, in many parts of the world, the opposite is the case. Rising expectations within some societies suggest it will be some time before there is any general admission that "they have never had it so good." Yet, even within these groups, it is being proved that the acquisition of more material goods is not of itself providing the answer. The pursuit of the external is indicating that the things for which people have craved are not to be found in the place where they are seeking them. Whether we are speaking of the dispossessed refugee or the millionaire, it is not money and material possessions alone that quench the deepest thirst for peace, happiness, health, and self-respect. That the more one gets, the more one wants, is true in every walk of life.

Even though a new assessment of reality is not yet general, there is, however, a shift of balance in thought and values. Prophecy about how this will evolve in the future does not rest so much on a projection of present material trends as on the fact that spirituality is the truth, and so inevitable. Its appearance through the mists of materiality is as inevitable as the dawn.

The Spiritual Truth

A sentence in Science and Health summarizes the new assessment of matter and material values. "The three great verities of Spirit, omnipotence, omnipresence, omniscience, — Spirit possessing all power, filling all space, constituting all Science, — contradict forever the belief that matter can be actual."[2]

A verity is a true thought or idea, and the power of a true thought lies in the thinking of that thought. This means the presence of the divine Mind as the only thinker of right thoughts. Power, presence, knowledge — the verities, or true ideas, of Spirit — comprise the whole of experience. In their spiritual significance, they are found to be aspects of the one Mind, and so remaining within Mind, and never externalised as modes of matter.

In human experience, these verities are illustrated as power or energy, communications, and knowledge. These are the human echo of the spiritual truth. The truth about what may appear as human power is the omnipotence of Spirit. The spiritual fact behind communications is omnipresence. And the escalation of human knowledge, now doubling about every three and a half years, hints at omniscience.

The Human Approximation

In each of these three areas, the escalation, proliferation, and extension that the last one hundred and fifty years have witnessed have been almost exponential. As developments have been less limited by a material, physical element, their efficacy has been increased. For example, the power which was once controlled by wind and muscle, involving considerable physical input to achieve scant results, is immeasurably enhanced by the use of nuclear energy, where the material element is slight yet the effect enormous. In communications, the physical effort involved in sending a runner or using smoke signals to convey a message, is replaced by modern methods where the minimum of physical apparatus has shrunk the world to a global village. And, in the field of knowledge, we see how the fastest growing industry today is that which deals with information.

What Is Causative?

To believe that these phenomena are material — that is, external to thought — is to invite an interpretation of the universe where technology is galloping out of control towards a destiny we cannot prevent. To see progress in terms of an enhancement of the capability of a human mind would be to attach to our experience of such developments the qualities and nature of that sense of everything. If the lens through which everything is viewed is the human mind, then everything will reflect that lens. On the other hand, if we begin, as scientific reasoning demands; if we survey all that is occurring with the lens, of the scientific I, then we perceive and experience the great verities as they really are. We see that what appears as human progress and an increase of human knowledge is actually the power, presence, and knowledge of God, less and less hidden by the limited vision of a human sense. Thus we understand that, instead of any increase in the wisdom of a so-called human mind, what is really happening is the decrease of this mind, or sense of things, because of the emergence of the eternal Truth. We then attach to our experience of these verities the character of the scientific lens, and place all under the shadow of the Almighty.

The Scientific View in Practice

Let us illustrate. The human experience of power can appear good or bad. An electric fire may warm the house, but it may blow up and fuse the lights. Nuclear energy may hold out prospects that are useful, yet its potential misuse is all too obvious. A piece of mechanism that controls power may fail. A friend was sitting in a car on a steep river bank reading, while her companions had gone for a walk. Suddenly the car started to move backward down to the river. This friend could not drive, but she knew something of the omnipotence of good, and declared aloud: "Being is safety." The car stopped immediately. When her companions returned, the driver found the brakes had failed, and there was no mechanical reason why the car should not have continued into the river. The verity of omnipotence did not depend on material brakes working or not. Safety and power depended on God.

In the field of communications, people can be brought closer together; distance and delay are overcome; the fact that omnipresence does not have to go somewhere or do something in order to be omnipresent is less hidden by material limits. Yet these same tools can appear as the means for intrusion, propaganda, and disinformation. And they can let us down by failing. Another friend had parted from her husband for some years. She was studying Science earnestly at the time, and one day her lodger announced that she was leaving. It seemed for a moment that a source of income, her baby sitter, her freedom to leave the house to give lessons and earn money, were all being removed. She was reminded that there can be no vacuums in the omnipresence of infinite Love and was told to decorate the vacant room. On the day the work finished, her husband telephoned after all this time. He returned, and a happy marriage ensued. The omnipresence of Love appeared as this simultaneity of good in the experience of both.

In terms of knowledge, human experience shows its potential usefulness and its misuse. So much, especially for those leaving college, seems to depend on the human acquisition of knowledge; so much seems lost because of lack of it. Yet omniscience is neither dependent on human brain nor material conditions, for it is inseparable from the other verities, omnipresence and omnipotence.

When still in business, it was necessary for me to get the input of some information from colleagues in four European countries. It was late afternoon and, because of the time zones, two of the offices were already closed. Calls to the other two were successful, and I knew that omniscience did not depend on anything outside of itself to be all-knowing. As the Bible verse puts it, "Known unto God [the divine Mind] are all his works from the beginning of the world."[3] Within the next half-hour, both the other two colleagues telephoned me, after their closing time, for reasons of their own. The required information was collected and the project completed.

The Viewpoint and the View

In each case, how we view a situation determines what we experience. What we may term a material state or a spiritual verity denotes levels of consciousness, not alternate facts. What seems palpably true at one level loses its verity at another. Only the interpretation of Principle, cause, presents the correct view. As we understand that all that is ever true is the spiritual verity, it will appear to us in its highest appreciable form. There is nothing wrong in lessening the toil of human existence through some new development in power. There is nothing incorrect in employing the latest means of communication to keep in touch with people. Nor is there anything unscientific in enjoying the vastly increased knowledge at our disposal. But, in each case, the appearing, the human illustration, must be recognised as a factor of the human, limited sense of things growing less, and not of this sense learning more. There can only be less, not better, obscuration.

In or Include

This leads us to an important two-letter word, namely, "IN." It is defined in Science and Health as "A term obsolete in Science if used with reference to Spirit, or Deity."[4] If you identify yourself as a finite bit of existence called a mortal, your universe will inevitably appear to be external to yourself, located *in* and at the whim of matter, or the duality of the human sense. Thus, you may find yourself *in* a job, an income or an age group, a class, a state of health, a home, a marriage, an aeroplane, or even just fix. And, except for the last, in which you are likely to remain, you can be out of the rest (like a job or a home) just as quickly. If an experience is seen in relation to the verities of being, you can realize that so long as the understanding or substance of the experience is recognised as the thought, or idea, of it, you are not *in* the appearance nor beholden to it. For example, to understand that an aeroplane, as a convenience, merely illustrates the spiritual verity of omnipresence, is to travel safely. You are not in, but exempt from, the human concept of it as a fallible bit of machinery. Mind, the scientific "I," is not in the idea it beholds and is never in any finite form.

But this divine Mind does include the right idea of transport, home, supply, activity, completeness, and so on. As the sum total of what Mind is knowing, man is the experience of this knowing. The requirement is just to let the idea, rather than concern about how it may appear, occupy consciousness. Good does not lie in the acquisition of material things but in letting the human misconception of good fade out before the verities we already include. Lack does not consist of the things the mortal does not have but lies in the failure to recognise that Mind always possesses the idea it includes. That which is included in consciousness comes forth as experience. But it is in what we value, and not what we have, that the test resides.

One Spiritual Universe

To seek a spiritual, or metaphysical, answer to what appear as material problems does not mean doing without all that makes life sweet and beautiful. Whatever is good, lovely, useful, or legitimate in our present experience presupposes the presence of God in some form. That which is baneful and discordant presupposes His absence and is inherent in the material view. "Being possesses its qualities before they are perceived humanly."[5] The loss of the limited, human sense of something does not remove a single quality of good but enhances it.

This is why neither a "Luddite" nor a monastic tendency is appropriate. The first, named after the workmen who, at the time of the Industrial Revolution, went about breaking up the machines they thought would deprive them of work, eschews all the usefulness that modern invention may offer. It throws the baby out with the bath-water . The second retreats from the ugliness of a material world into its cell, whilst leaving the problems of materialism outside. Both attitudes assume two worlds: a material and a spiritual. But this is not the case. There is one infinite universe which is wholly spiritual when seen as "I" see it. From this higher altitude of perception, the apparent duality of material experience dissolves. The so-called human mind, with the upside-down view of the one universe that *it* includes, yields to the correct interpretation of everything from the standpoint of the scientific "I." The misstatement of the universe as material gives place to the scientific statement of being as Spirit, or "*spiritual* consciousness alone."[6]

As eternal Truth asserts itself in consciousness, the clouds of ignorance inherent in the material view become so palpably untenable as to be self-seen and so self-destroyed. As the translation of the misstatement back into its original language, Mind, takes place, being is found to be spiritual and harmonious.Then we see that the stuff of which everything is made is thought, the consciousness of the divine Mind. We enjoy our present, subjective being in all its safety, permanence, and inexhaustible good. Matter is expendable: the medium becomes redundant, but the idea remains. This is inevitable. One way or the other, "Truth will out," because Truth, as a synonym for God, is that which IS.

6

Science and Religion

Science commits suicide when it adopts a creed.
Thomas Huxley

Churches may inform the minds of men, but they
cannot enforce them.
John Owen

A scientifically spiritual perspective, as the phrase implies, necessarily embraces a fresh interpretation of both science and religion. In the broadest sense, we are talking about knowledge and that to which we bind back daily experience and behaviour. This means a new look at everything of which we can be conscious.

Understanding and Belief

The order of Science demands that reasoning and inter-pretation take place from the standpoint of the divine Principle. In any science this is the correct way in which to reach a conclusion. This is because Mind, the causative Principle, includes its idea but is not included by it. To begin from any other standpoint is to assume that there is some platform outside that science from which reasoning can take place. In the divine Science of being, which must of necessity be an infinite Science, such a standpoint is impossible. Truth, or that which is, can be fully known only from the standpoint of Truth itself. There is nothing outside of that which is. Only God can know God, because only I can know what I AM.

Religious history tends to be the record of a different approach and consists of the attempt to know and understand God, or Principle, from the standpoint of man, or idea. While the truth is the centre of all religion, the attempt to approach Truth from outside it results in a choice of many paths to follow. It is the certainty that there is an ultimate reality, or Truth, that brings strength and comfort to the traveller along these paths. Indeed, as Einstein said, "Without the belief in the inner harmony of the world, there could be no science." It is the move from an awareness of some inner harmony to a scientific understanding of the Principle of harmony that is pointed to by religious history. At some point, however, belief has to yield to understanding which, in turn, is a quality evolved from Principle and not a goal for human search. Belief stays in the realm of opinion; Truth, or understanding, is experience. Truth cannot be satisfactorily believed — only understood.

So long as belief is unchallenged, there is little incentive to rethink its basis. This was the case within the old religious scheme of things. The sciences, such as they were, remained subordinate to religion — something that Galileo and others found to their cost. When the rationalism of science first took over the minds of men, following the Renaissance, it was at the expense of religion. The passage from a religious to a scientific age brought separation, not fusion. Because religion could not be properly explained in the terms of science, it had to fall back on mystery, superstition, and an assumption that God had, so to speak, to be taken on trust, since one could not expect to explain Him in the terms of the unbeliever.

The Rejection of the Omniscience of Science

It is only in comparatively recent times that two developments have taken place, both of enormous importance. The first is that the escalation and pace of scientific discovery have now brought a questioning of its purpose and usefulness. In earlier times, when the milestones of major discovery were more widely spaced, it was easier to accept the discovery without being overwhelmed by it. For example, the acceptance of Arabic notation or the invention of the printing press each stood alone in its time. People could make up their minds about their importance and learn to live with them. Moreover, there was a moral and religious continuum, provided by the church, against which their value could be assessed. Today, this has changed. The interval between drawing board and product is shortened; the division and subdivision of knowledge into specialized compartments proliferate; and there is no longer the same religious yardstick against which to measure the desirability of "progress."

The second development coincides with an instinctive feeling that all is not well in a world that is left in the hands of the physical scientists. An element of the moral, the intuitive, the arational, the poetic, is lacking. A computer can tell you, in a fraction of a second, the shortest distance between two points on your journey. But it cannot tell you that, if you make a detour through a garden in the spring, this will make your journey seem shorter. The value of the detour is the exposure to beauty. A heightened sense of beauty is essential to seeing God. It is the most tangible of all aspects of God as Love and must permeate all aspects of experience.

As in many other areas, there appears to be an imbalance as the old order is questioned and a new one seen but not grasped. Physical science has shaken the basis of conventional religious thought but has not offered a replacement for the religious feeling that supported churchgoers. This sense of imbalance is now coinciding with a mental move towards finding a reconciliation between science and religion — a move that finds support from sages, mystics, and scientists alike.

Speaking aboard the battleship Missouri, in September 1945, General Douglas MacArthur said, "Military alliances, balances of power, League of Nations, all in turn have failed. We have had our last chance. The problem basically is theological and involves a spiritual recrudescence and improvement of human character, that will synchronize with our almost matchless advance in science."

New Views from East and West

A general leavening of thought is reflected in an awakened interest in the teachings of the East as well as new ideas in Christianity. This is partly because Eastern thought has never lost its sense of balance between the world of consciousness and that of appearance, as has been the case in the West. A religious meaning is vested in the simplest actions of daily life, and the more cerebral, aggressively material, and male-dominated approach of the West does not make a great impression. Conventional Christianity, on the other hand, had never recognised the fundamental importance of consciousness, and has been stamped with concern for a personal God and personal human lives. The breakaway from this conventional thought is reflected in the rapid growth of fundamentalism in Christianity, even though the personal preoccupation remains. Whether or not the accusation of emotion is justified, it is a fact that many people, including a large proportion of young, find something that they can FEEL and not just know intellectually.

Of course, part of the attraction of much of the teaching that is being brought from the East is that it is not formally structural or hierarchical; it does not demand a uniformity of practice, nor is it hedged about with creeds and formalism. Its appeal is to free thought, and its bigotry is minimal. It can be noted, too, that there is a greater willingness on the part of Eastern teachers to quote the teaching of Christ Jesus than there is by Western clerics to give tribute to the wisdom of the Buddha.

This seems a pity, because something true has to be all-embracing. There is not an Eastern and a Western truth any more than there is an English and a Chinese application of mathematics. While it is true that some of the modern deviations from the teaching of the Vedas are as great as the deviation of many professed Christians from the teachings of Christ Jesus, the sublimity of the original writings remains and cannot be gainsaid.

A breath of fresh air came with an article by the then dean of St. Paul's Cathedral in London, Dr. W.R. Mathews, in which he wrote:

> Is it not strange how loyalty to our own Church can blind us to the triumphs of the spirit of Christ outside of it? We are so sure that we are in the right place that we can hardly conceive others may be as near to God in their different tabernacles.
>
> Yet, though they follow not with us, they are perhaps casting out the devils of lust and selfishness and despair with power greater than our own. They may not have the approval of the ecclesiastical authorities but they have the witness of the Spirit.

Writing in similar vein, the late Dom Bede Griffiths said, "The narrow-mindedness which has divided the Christian churches from one another has also divided the Christian religion from other religions. Each religion must learn to discern its essential truth and to reject its cultural and historical limitations."

Christ Jesus, like other great religious teachers, gave mankind a religion — a way of life but not a church organization — that was based on Love. To his immediate followers, a church was just somewhere where people who loved each other could meet and learn more about God. The essence of their religion did not reside in a temple but in the practice of the truth they knew in daily life and in healing the sick. This persisted until, with the passing of time, ecclesiasticism took over, and soon nearly smothered, the ideas the Master taught and practiced in the desert, on a hillside, in a boat, and as he went about his daily business.

The Post-Christian Age

Today a new dimension — a scientific one — has been added to the religion of Love that Christ Jesus taught. In what might be called a post-Christian age, a new scientific rationalism is removing mystery and superstition, but in a way that confirms rather than eschews the essence of religious thought. As this takes place, there would seem to be two lines that have to be pursued.

The first is to let a bigness of heart and a breadth of vision find the eternal Truth that lies beneath the forms in which it appears. It should not be surprising to discover that Truth does shine through and, one might say, despite the creeds and doctrine that often hide it with vain repetition.

The second is that, while compassion and vision can bring tolerance and peace between religious factions, it will be a scientific, rather than a religious ecumenical, approach that brings true unity of Spirit. It is from the scientific basis of only one Mind, or Ego, and not from the basis of trying humanly to bring unity out of a premise of many religious minds, that the correct interpretation and experience of being are gained.

Science and Christianity

The application of the word "Science" to religion is not contradictory, for it points to the spiritual understanding of being rather than the human opinions which constitute the imperfect view of all that is. If there is one, infinite Mind, then one cannot have a foundation that says that either science or religion is, or is not, true. Science and art, Principle and Love, justice and mercy walk hand in hand. Principle must be expressed as Science, or "exact knowledge," and a world of ideas should be no less exact than a world of objects and things. The fact that Spiritual or Divine Science shows forth the exactitude, precision, order, and legality of being through spiritual, rather than material, laws does not make it any less a science. On the contrary, it rightly embraces all science or knowledge, since any human, physical science is, of necessity, partial and confined to some discipline.

Until now there has been more or less unquestioning reliance on physical law. When we get up in the morning, we do not for a moment question gravity. But Spiritual Science is the law of universal good in every detail of Life. When religion is seen to be operating at the level of Science, we find that there is a whole range of spiritual laws as valid and present as any that we thought were material. It is necessary only to learn how to use these laws.

To speak of the Science of Christianity, or Christian Science, as the term which conveys the laws by which the Master Christian worked, and which he put into practice in his ministry, would seem equally logical. Either he was demonstrating eternal laws — and the promise that those who believed on him would do the same works indicates this — or his mission was a dispensation that was limited to a place and a period and thus of little relevance to us today. Without the means of practicing what he taught, Christianity would be shorn of its primal purpose, and "the Way" would be without signposts. But, on the other hand, if what he taught and proved were really spiritual, eternal laws, then they had to transcend the dogma of both East and West and replace religious differences of opinion with the universality and freedom of Science. Then it would be seen that this Science could be studied, understood, and practiced by Christians, Buddhists, and others alike, just as no one could be barred from access to the laws of mathematics.

True Ecumenicalism

This Spiritual or Christian Science is the fulfillment, not the denial, of what Christ Jesus taught, for it shows how to reinstate the lost element of spiritual healing that marked his ministry. It unites with the Jew and the Mohammedan, who believe in one God yet who would distinguish between the personal Jesus and the Christ, Truth, that he taught. And it fulfills — fills full — the finest teaching of the East, in which the mental nature of everything is recognised, but the illusory nature of a material world tends to be set aside rather than redeemed. The good news of Science is not that you focus on illusion, let alone ignore it, but that you translate it back into its original meaning and substance. Then, incidentally, the human sense of things appears increasingly beautiful, elevated, and abundant, though not necessarily in the way that human thought may outline. The extremes of either following "holy" men, or trying to get some human result in the way one humanly decides, are avoided. The human betterment is incidental to the fading out of ignorance. As Christ Jesus said, "Seek ye first the kingdom of God and his righteousness; and all these things shall be added unto you."[1] You cannot have "All" *and* something else, even if that apparent something is then called an illusion. Mind contains no illusion, and the presence of Mind is the Saviour from even a belief in something else. The false sense, the upside down view, is translated back into Mind and so redeemed.

It would seem arguable that, rather than witnessing a return to teaching that has been buried for a long time, the natural development of thought is towards a new plateau where the religious good of both East and West is fulfilled in a Spiritual Science that transcends both this sense of good and the physical sciences as well. Unless the world of appearances is recognised as the one and only world, though misconceived, and unless these appearances are translated back into Mind, one will always be left with something other than the Truth that is to be ignored, swept aside, or given at least temporary power and status. Thus, the theological ghost of preparing for future perfection, rather than starting from its presence now, will not be laid, and salvation will continue to be dependent on the human effort of Christians or the cycles of time of Eastern thought. The Science of being proclaims perfection now.

The Impact of Christianity

Despite the shortfall in the practice of Christian teaching, it is evident that, where it has been embraced in the world in any degree, there too has been the greatest progress for mankind. Nor is this just questionable, material progress but reform and enlightenment in social, civil, and political law; standards of hygiene; the removal of human drudgery and the growth in quality of life; care for the environment; new aspirations and exploration; and freedom of thought and action. The maps of religious and human emancipation coincide. "Thus it is that our ideas of divinity form our models of humanity."[2]

The marriage between Science and Christianity demands

not only scientifically correct reasoning but also a corresponding growth in Christian character. This entails, as Jesus pointed out, the degree of self-abnegation that allows no personal sense to obscure the divine nature. "It was the consummate naturalness of Truth in the mind of Jesus, that made his healing easy and instantaneous."[3] For good to be natural requires a close acquaintanceship with good. The light shines through clearest when the window pane is clear. Then people come to the light, not the window pane. It is the light that lightens the darkness. This "unselfing" of life and purpose has been the demand of all the world's great religions.

A Universal Science

If there were no Principle, or Science, of being, the universe would be a state of infinite, eternal chaos and self-destruction. Perhaps this is how it might first seem to the superficial observer. But, in Science, ignorance and superficiality do not assimilate Truth, whereas Truth does displace ignorance. And, if there is a Science of being, then it has to be eternal, universal, omnipresent, and demonstrable, as well as independent of human opinion.

Such a Science is no more the monopoly of any group of persons than is mathematics or physics. No priesthood can control, ration, censor, or direct it. No material organization can embody it. No creed or doctrine can encapsulate it. It is as free for all to use as the air we breathe. Individuals, with the spoken or written word, may throw some fresh and useful slant on Science. They may help the student, in the same way as the itinerant teachers did in olden times. Meetings, discussions, forms of material cohesion, may be temporarily useful. They may reassure and strengthen the enquirer. But no more. A science is to be lived, for it is experience. There is no substitute for this. A science cannot be cemented into dogma and form.

Its usefulness lies in the degree to which it is lived, practiced, and proved, and this is up to the individual. The individual practitioner of Science relates to his Principle, never to person.

Science means knowledge, or understanding, and understanding is Principle, or God, in self-expression. It is as universal, as old, as present as God Himself, for it is the knowledge of that which is. Such knowledge cannot be humanly appropriated. We read in Science and Health, "If God, the All-in-all, be the creator of the spiritual universe, including man, then everything entitled to a classification as truth, or Science, must be comprised in a knowledge or understanding of God, for there can be nothing beyond illimitable divinity."[4]

This knowledge of God is for all. It does not delineate a path *to* holiness, or wholeness, but is the way *of* wholeness itself. As thought is in relation to the divine Mind, it drops its human limitations. It finds release from the prison of a personal ego; release from the restrictions of ecclesiastical, social, political, medical, and other material laws; freedom from the whole of sense-existence, or life cognised through the five physical senses; emancipation from the inadequacy, penury, disappointment, fear, frustration, and ugliness that accompany so-called existence apart from God. Science, like Truth, is freedom's selfhood. Life that is one with God is Life as the divine Mind knows and experiences it. It is this God-being that constitutes the Science we live and practice. No one, anywhere, is beyond the pale of this Life; no one is debarred from its practice any more than anyone could be prevented from practicing mathematics. The laws of God, operating as all true consciousness, comprise the Science, the understanding, of being, which, as we shall see, is the real man.

7

What Do We Mean by God ?

*I am that which is. I am that is, that was,
and that will be. No mortal man has raised
my veil. He is solely from Himself, and all
things owe their being to Him.*
                    The Mission of Moses
                    Schiller

*It is impossible to understand God without
understanding the unreality of matter .*
                    Tolstoi

The fusion of science and religion into a new, spiritually scientific perspective necessarily demands a fresh assessment first of what we mean by God, and then of man. On the subject of the New Age spirituality, Mark Satin wrote, "This is now regarded as a very irreligious age. But perhaps it means merely that the mind is moving from one stage to another. Both polytheism and monotheism have done their work. The next stage is not a belief in many gods. It is not a belief in one God. It is not a belief at all — not a conception in the intellect. It is an extension of consciousness so that we may *feel* God or, if you will, an experience of harmony, the experience of unity lost at the in-break of self-consciousness." The search for an intelligent and intelligible cause and the innate love of good are as strong today as ever.

It would seem, however, that the word "God" tends in general to be reserved for Sundays, and does not readily form part of the vocabulary of polite society. Yet, if God is the term for Truth, or that which *is*, and so *all* that is, then the avoidance of this subject can only confine conversation to a range of matters that, by the same definition, are not. It should be possible to think of God in terms of the whole of Life, and not just in a theological context.

A New Interpretation

Our traditional concepts of God need to be refined, so that what belonged to the unquestioning faith of an earlier era can meet the demands of a rational approach that is consistent with a scientific age. In the second chapter we explored the idea that God, or Truth, can be known only from the standpoint of Truth itself. This is because the acceptance of any other standpoint has to presuppose some place outside of, and additional to, reality. We would be saying that it is possible to understand the infinite from somewhere apart from infinity. And how can there be such a place?

A personal interpretation of God will reflect the state of thought and the level of inspiration of the interpreter. This interpretation attributes personal characteristics to God which may range from anger to mercy. This may change as well as differ from other interpretations. This is why the correct and scientific interpretation of God has to be from the standpoint of the Principle that is God. This also is why, in the great religions of the world, God has been referred to as unknown, undefinable, nameless, indescribable. The nearest any personal approach has come to defining Deity has been to describe the way in which it is expressed.

Men can define God by the qualities that express God, just as we would define a flower by the qualities that express it. For example, the feeling of good, or love, or beauty points to something behind this feeling, which we call a God that is Love. The awareness of order, law, and intelligent government points to a God who is the undeviating Principle of the universe. But, ultimately, no human interpretation can do other than approximate reality. It will always be incomplete, because it places the observer apart from what is being observed. Thus, any attempt to understand God from such a standpoint tends to define what God is not, rather than what He is. People can say that God is not this or that more easily than they can explain what God is. This is because only God can know God. Principle is not in that which expresses it, just as the artist is not in his painting.

The Refining Concept

Over the centuries, religious history has witnessed an important move which has taken the form of worship away from polytheism, or the worship of many gods, to monotheism, or the worship of one God. Central to Judaic-Christian thought has been the great statement, "The Lord our God is one Lord."[1] In fact, the line of history is not altogether distinct, for the gods of a materialistic society — video, VR (Virtual Reality), material riches, and so on — are at least as demanding of the heart, and mind, and soul of man as any pagan idols. Gods are everything to which men attribute power. A new trend, nevertheless, is apparent in this post-Christian era, where there is growing disinclination to worship anything. This is not necessarily because there is any less awareness of, or interest in, some intelligent, governing cause. Rather is it because human theories about this cause, or Principle, are no longer convincing, and what is sometimes called "the God within" seems more credible than any man-projected Deity. Truth is deemed to be experience, not belief, and the traditional media for trying to approach and know Truth are being discarded.

The Scientific Definition

Science and Health defines God as "The great I AM; the

all-knowing, all-seeing, all-acting, all-wise, all-loving, and eternal; Principle; Mind; Soul; Spirit; Life; Truth; Love; all substance; intelligence."[2] Five of these synonyms (Soul; Spirit; Life; Truth; Love) have long been used by Christian churches as names for God, and are to be found in the Bible. So, too, is the word "mind," though Science capitalizes this term and refers to the one Mind as the only I or Ego. Some other religions have also called God by this name. And the term "Principle," though new, is implicit in reference to a first cause that governs every manifestation of itself.

All these terms are, of course, familiar without the capitalization in their use to describe personal behaviour. People readily admit that they have a mind and a soul; that they are alive; and that they know about love. They consider themselves to be persons of principle who speak the truth, and that the spirit of what they say and do shows more of its substance than the letter. But, at a human level, we all know that all these qualities appear to have an opposite. The same person can find himself or herself in a situation where he or she becomes unprincipled, unloving, untruthful, and even unalive or dead. This is because any attribute that is seen through the distorting lens of the human mind will portray the duality of that mind.

By capitalizing them, these terms are seen to be synonyms for, rather than attributes of, God. They become nouns, and so refer to the unchanging name, or nature, of that which is self-existent and self-expressed. They refer to the source or origin of all that is strong and tender, uncompromising yet gentle, pure and perfect. They define the essence of reality, or that which is being, and so that which I AM.

When we cease to think and talk *about* God; when we stop referring to God as He or Him, thus objectifying our sense of the infinite, we have to come to an inescapable conclusion. Either these synonyms define for us the nature and quality of our own seeing and being, or they are irrelevant. Either the divine Mind and Life constitute our knowing and living here and now or, so far as we are concerned, they remain as remote from practical experience as any man-like potentate that symbolized God in the past. Either Truth operates as our own truthful seeing or, again, we might as well not use the term.

We can be specific. If Truth, the evidence of God with us, is true, then how do we regard another's behaviour? Do we react to it through sympathy or anger? Or do we maintain the yardstick of what is true from the standpoint of Truth itself, and let that, rather than the picture of another, occupy our thought? How do we regard the news items that reach us through the public media? Do we correct our view of the disasters, crime, sorrows that are presented, or do we accept them and so give them further pretense to life? This "putting a sieve" over our thinking is a full-time job. It means that we constantly relate thought back to Principle, or God's law in operation, and so to Truth, not to phenomena.

Similarly, to know *as* the divine Mind (for, remember, we cannot think *about* the Mind we have) means that Mind with us precludes the thoughts and experience of a so-called human mind. This consciousness in turn assures that Life is with us, in all its changeless continuity, freshness, colour, because "to be spiritually minded is life and peace," whereas carnal mindedness is death. To love, not as a capricious or selfish display of human emotion but as the consistent awareness of the harmony, beauty, and perfection of being, is to let Love loving *be* the nature and texture of our Life.

Not "He" but "I"

Every synonym of God has to begin with the words I AM. We have seen that the capacity to know correctly is the capacity of pure Mind, and it is our relation to this Mind, as the only source and condition of true consciousness, that allows that which emanates from and as this Mind to prefix its capacity to know with the word "I." God does not say "He is," nor does the Mind we call God countenance another capacity to know. God is no more "He" than beauty is "over there." Consciousness that is one with the divine Mind can know only in terms of I and My. Referring back to the statement by Mark Satin at the beginning of this chapter, he specifies a " next stage" as "the experience of unity lost at the in-break of self-consciousness." Science restores that unity by conceptually dissolving the self-consciousness, or limited ego, which is the basic stumbling block. In this way only, do "we know even as we are known" and find why it is that, in Love, the words " mine" and " thine" become obsolete.

None of the above suggests in any way that man usurps the role of Deity. The divine Mind is the only I or Ego, and scientific thought is necessarily from the standpoint of "I." As idea, man is constituted of the thoughts of Mind, and the sum total of existence is God and His thoughts. Man is manifestation, expression, reflection, but there is nothing to say "I am man." It is man's Mind that speaks and says "I AM," and what is spoken is the word of God, not the word of man. The idea of God, though one with the Mind that is God, has no capacity to usurp the Mind that conceives the idea.

It is the educated belief that there is a capacity to say I — and therefore to know, live, and love — separate from the Principle, that would make gods out of men. This was surely the symbolism of the allegory of the fall in the

Garden of Eden, for the partaking of a false or illicit knowledge presumed that there was a capacity to know that was resident in man. It is anything but humble to claim a separate life or mind from the infinite. The eviction of the arrogant claim inherent in the serpent's promise that "ye shall be as gods knowing good and evil"[3] — the claim that this knowledge could enter the divine consciousness — was, and is, merited.

Neither human self-abasement nor self-aggrandizement ever leaves the basis or belief in a separate, mortal self. To acknowledge a separate life, even in the service of God, is to dishonour God. Man, as image, is not a knower or a thinker, for one Mind means one knower and one thinker. "For God to know, is to be;"[4] and what God knows, He is. What I know, I AM. In the oneness of knowing and being, or cause and effect, "God" and "man" are found to be educational terms. In reality, there are not two entities but, rather, two aspects of one substance, one consciousness, one Life.

We thus find that, when we have said God, we have also said man, for this All which we call God is both Principle and idea. It is not possible to have the first without the second; to have Mind without its consciousness; to have Life and Love without the functions that represent them and so complete the nature and wholeness of Deity. God's knowledge, understanding, awareness, and appreciation of Himself constitute the evidence to God that He is and what He is. Man and the universe are really God's self-identification, not as matter, but as consciousness or idea. As consciousness, idea is as necessary to its Principle, or cause, as Principle is to its idea, or effect. Neither could exist without the other. This is why Jesus could say, "I and my Father are one,"[5] and it is for the same reason that Science and Health states, "Principle and its idea is one, and this one is God, omnipotent, omniscient, and omnipresent Being, and His reflection is man and the universe."[6]

God Expressed as Man

Man, then, is not a separate entity that knows God, but the knowing that God is doing. Man is not a knower of Truth, but is all that Truth is knowing. Man is not something that loves God, but is the love of Love, for "We love him, because he first loved us."[7] Nor does man live a good life but is the living that Life itself is demonstrating. Mind's reflection is Mind's identity, the same entity as the word implies, and never separate from that which is its life, substance, and intelligence.

Being, then, consists of the consciousness of harmony called God and man; the duet of joy and praise, sung with a single voice, with God the singer and man the song. Everything that is going on is God being. Principle is unfolding as the whole of experience. Its idea includes the full manifestation of itself. That which unfolds will appear in a form and a language that are appreciable at any moment. It will appear as all that is good, useful, bountiful, and beautiful. By whatever name we call this appearance, it has to be God being, for there is nothing else to be.

God is the whole of existence. This does not imply the pantheistic belief that God is in matter or evil. In a universe of thought, matter is found to be insubstantial. We have seen that it consists of thought impressions of a mind that is not the divine. The universe of the divine Mind consists solely of ideas, because Mind can originate only thought. Spiritual forms are outlined thought – outlined in the sense of being distinct and identifiable, but not limited. The inversion or misconception of these forms by the lens of the human mind presents them as material and having the character of that mind. The storm in the Indian port was such an inversion, yet it had no validity. It was an impression of chaos without substance. It was an appearance, mirage, without reality.

It is in this way that we can answer the reasonable question, If God is good and omnipotent, how can He allow evil? This issue will be dealt with in Chapter 17, "The Knowledge of Good and Evil." The question is still a left-over from theology, which tries to explain God in terms of what is cognised through the five senses. It is a form of the age-old search to explain the origin of evil, which begins from the premise that evil is an existing reality with an origin. If God is a man-like potentate, then it is necessary to explain the impotence that would permit an opposite to His own nature. If God knew this opposite, it would have to imply that a knowledge of evil was part of the Mind of God. No doctrine of free-will or original sin would make such an implication conceivable. But, if God is Principle, then that Principle can no more know, include, or permit a deviation from itself than can the principle of mathematics. The conclusion has to be that neither evil nor the mind that is aware of it forms part of the consciousness of God, any more than the shadows that hide the light are perceptible to that which is aware only of light. Thus evil, in all its forms, is to be classified as the experience of a mind that is itself mere supposition. Escape from it lies not in fighting it but in the consciousness of infinite good, or God, that never knew it.

Spiritual Translation

To see and commune with God as the whole of our being means that, whatever the form in which experience appears to us, it is the idea, and not the appearance, that is our concern. The Love that is God, for instance, may be recognisable as what is called a companion, a warm house, a kindly neighbour, but while Love constitutes all that appears in this way, the appearance itself is not Love. The beauty of a sunset, when interpreted as consciousness instead of as material coruscations in the sky, allows the Principle to declare, "What beauty I AM." The majesty of the mountains, the abundance of leaves on the tree, the grace of an animal's walk, when separated mentally from their material accompaniments, allow the I that is this Principle to say, " What majesty, abundance, grace I AM." And it is when the substance of everything is understood to remain in the consciousness of the divine Mind, that the duality, vulnerability, and ephemeral nature that are attached to the perception of the same things by the human senses are removed.

The material accompaniments fade out as more of the underlying substance appears, and the human mind, with the misconceptions it includes, yields to the divine. We do not decry or belittle or ignore a single thing that unfolds: we translate it back into its original, Mind. Even the so-called bad is seen to be but an inversion of that which is true, just as the negative in photography shows, by reversal, the positive. "If God, the All-in-all, be the creator of the spiritual universe, including man, then everything entitled to a classification as truth, or Science, must be comprised in a knowledge or understanding of God, for there can be nothing beyond illimitable divinity."[8]

Man as Divine Consciousness

It is in knowing God that we find man, for such knowing is really God's own knowledge of Himself. In this knowledge the pains and sorrows of a finite mind and life fade out.

For example, the knowledge or consciousness of God's abundance is the idea of abundance called abundant man.

The consciousness of God's completeness is the idea of completeness called complete man. The consciousness of God's activity is the idea of activity called active man. And the consciousness of God's wholeness is the idea of wholeness called whole, or healthy, man. In every case, God is identified as the idea that expresses Him.

A friend, who was a life-long student of Science, had been in the most acute pain for several days and nights. She was lying on her bed, hardly able to think. She gasped, "Dear God, I am so grateful to know this is not Your experience." Instantly she was free of the pain, and she rose from her bed completely well. It was not the experience of God, so it was not that of man, since they existed as one Mind, one Life, one being. The mistaken sense of being, like a mistake in mathematics, vanished before the Truth into its native nothingness. In this case, the student knew enough to understand that the impetus to prayer is not just how to get rid of pain, for pain is simply an experience of a so-called human mind. She knew that Truth is the same before, during, and after an apparent struggle. Prayer was the simple acknowledgement of the truth, despite what the human was feeling. If one understands the Science of being, then one cannot be taken in by the picture of struggle. The issue is bigger than the experience.

God, then, is the term we use for the whole of Life, your Life; the whole of Mind, your Mind or consciousness; the whole of Truth, of Love, the whole of what I accept as the I of My being and the experience that is being. It is all-ness, known from the standpoint of that which is All. It is that which I AM, where all thought of identity as a mortal "i" or ego has been forever unknown. It antedates the whole process of mortal history, grasping in the hand of omnipotence the eternal now.

8

How Do We Identify Man ?

*In our hearts and minds there now doth work not
that spirit which is the influence and animal
intelligence of the world, but the divine Spirit,
and this it is which reveals to us those things that
are bestowed on man by God... The materially
minded man, who thinks through the senses, is
totally and utterly ignorant of God's spiritual
messages... It is as spiritual beings, and not
carnal, that we possess the mind of Christ.*

> *St. Paul from the Trenches*
> *I Corinthians 2*
> *Gerald Warre Cornish*

*Man becomes less and less in time and space
and more and more in comprehension.*

> *Prof. Harlow Shapley*
> *Harvard Astronomer*

As we have noted, a reassessment of what we mean by
"God" implies a new look at the way we identify man.
Because we are talking about a universe that consists fundamentally of thoughts, or consciousness, the interpretation of man as material physique cannot be adequate. This
does not mean that, at a certain level of thought, man is
not just what he seems — a creature with two arms and
legs. But it does suggest that, if we were to look at things
from a different standpoint, the view might be quite different.

The Mask of Personality

The search for identity preoccupies mankind. This search always begins by accepting the definition of man which is afforded by the five physical senses. This portrays man as a physical personality, recognisable as a physical identity, and subject to all the limitations, inadequacies, and frustrations that are inherent in this view. It is no wonder that people seek a higher selfhood but, because the attempt is made from the starting point of the physical personality, they find too often the truth that a fountain cannot rise higher than its source.

To assess man from a somewhat higher standpoint allows us to understand that, behind the mask of personality (and mask, indeed, is what this word originally meant), there lie qualities that are also recognisable and that make up our sense of someone's individuality. These qualities do transcend the limitations of corporeality. The beauty of character, for example, does not fade but is enhanced with advancing years. Courage, generosity, dignity, and all that portrays a distinct character are not fettered by the flesh. At moments of great demand, when someone rises to the height of his or her individual character, it is this, rather than any physical feature, that is remembered. And, the same would be true of those we know as artists, who may have lived centuries ago, but whose work in music, painting, and writing identifies them to us now.

In human experience, however, it would appear that not only do physicality and qualities of character unite in one person, but also all the opposites of existence seen through the lens of the human mind. Man appears to be an arena where good and evil, life and death, health and sickness meet and mingle. In this manner, identity is given to the negative, and the experience of the positive reality is curtailed by limiting it to person. To obtain an even higher view of man, without the duality of human experience, a new viewpoint is needed, even if the conclusions that result are quite contrary to what we have been educated to believe is true.

Three Steps in Finding Spiritual Identity

As always, scientific reasoning on any subject has to be from cause to effect. The recognition that Mind is cause leads to a number of conclusions. The first is that the off-spring of Mind are thoughts, or ideas. Mind is the parent of thought only, for the nature of that which expresses Mind cannot depart from that Mind in nature or character. The fruits of the Spirit do not depart from the spiritual nature of the tree that bears them. Moreover, these fruits, or qualities, are the only link with the Mind and the Life that we call God.

The second, and perhaps obvious, conclusion is that thoughts do not appear without a Mind to think them. In the analogy of the Cheshire cat, you cannot have something so absurd as a smile without a smiler! What is important to note is that the consciousness and substance of a thought, or idea, are not in the idea but in the Mind that has it. The substance, life, and capacity of an idea never leave the Mind that forms them, any more than your likeness in a mirror can be or do anything separate from you in front of the mirror. The original always has its reflection with it, and the reflection, in turn, is subject to the original.

A third, and this time less obvious, conclusion is that the same Mind cannot conceive thoughts that are both consistent and inconsistent with its character. Despite the human appearance of the mingling of opposites, there can be no such mingling in the original. Pure Mind cannot include the knowledge of an opposite to itself. If it could do so, then this opposite would have to form part of the eternal nature, and we would not only be unable to overcome the bane of human existence, but we would also have to ascribe full responsibility for it to God.

Whatever the appearance of mingling in the arena of human personality, Science could not admit the possibility of this occurring. It would therefore follow that the appearance of an arena is true only within certain mental terms of reference, which themselves are unknown to the divine Mind.

Light and Rays

An illustration of the foregoing can be gained by considering the appearance of rays of light. In physics, there are no rays. Their appearance is formed by impurity or dust in the atmosphere. This gives the impression that the substance of light and the substance of dust mingle to form rays. The purer the atmosphere, the more the impression of rays recedes, and the ultimate is pure light with no rays.

Within the human, inaccurate terms of reference, these rays might be likened to human personalities. It is not surprising that the allegory relates that Adam was "formed... of the dust of the ground."[1] It is easy to equate the merely physical characteristics of mortal men and women with the dust, with all that is ephemeral and ultimately unreal. It is harder to understand that the often fine qualities of the individual, human character cannot in themselves be attributed to and so limited by person. Harder, that is, unless we keep our scientific starting point and insist that, no matter what the physical evidence, like can only produce like.

In his exemplary life, Christ Jesus made the distinction between thinking that was from above — from the divine

Mind — and thinking that emanated from the carnal mind or what he termed "a liar, and the father of it."[2] He understood and proved that the good in human experience was always the good of God, appearing despite and not because of the educated belief it was human. Likewise the bad was just this lie, and so no part of reality. He referred to the tares and wheat which, at the time of harvest, would be separated, because they never belonged to each other. At the same time, he emphasised that this harvest was now, and not at some future date. In the analogy of the rays of light, it was the removal of the dust, or tares, or that which was from beneath, that brought into clearer view the light, or wheat, or that which was from above and always present.

The highest love we can show towards our fellow man is to see him, so to speak, as light rather than a ray; to separate our concept of man from the limitations of personhood, and so to distinguish in our own thought that which seems to come from beneath and is the temporal misconception, from that which is from above and is the eternal manifestation of Truth. It means not accepting a picture that, at best, is true only within its own terms of reference. This is how we love our neighbour as ourself, for it is our own thought that is barred from accepting a concept of man that would defile the pure image of his Maker. Christ Jesus made this clear when he said, "Inasmuch as ye have done it unto one of the least of these my brethren, ye have done it unto me."[3] What we accept of another becomes part of what we accept as I.

A sculptor has in mind his ideal. Taking the raw material, he chips away at all that would hide this ideal. He does not pay attention to the chips, which are discarded as having nothing to do with the reality he is bringing out. He continues his work until this reality is revealed. Thus we all bring out our ideal.

True Identification

It is now that we can return to the basic question, namely, How do we identify man in Science? If he is not just personality, nor even a human individuality where good and evil mingle, what is man? Science says that "we know no more of man as the true divine image and likeness, than we know of God."[4] In knowing God, Principle, we find man or, to use a better word which has no physical connotation, we find the manifestation of this Principle. Just as a rose is known by the qualities that express it — its scent, colour, shape — so that you are aware of the identity of a rose and can say, "This is what a rose is," so the qualities and thoughts that express the Father-Principle inform you of what you are as this Parent's image and likeness. It was this approach that allowed Jesus to say, "He that hath seen me hath seen the Father."[5]

We can look at some of these qualities, though there will be many more, and obtain an indication of the true nature of man. The wisdom and intelligence of Mind ensure the wise and intelligent experience of man; the strength and presence of Spirit constitute the strong and spiritual nature of man; the purity of Soul is the purity of its idea, whereas the order, law, and continuity of Principle guarantee the order and legality of Principle's ever-unfolding idea; Life is expressed in many ways, including freshness, colour, interest, and fun, whilst Truth is manifest as the integrity, indivisibility, and freedom of its expression. And Love never loses sight of the loveliness and harmony of its own being. All these ideas, these fruits of the Spirit, are from above, and so "against such there is no law."

Mind, Love, Truth, Life — each of the synonymous terms for God — surveys the beauty of the ideas that constitute its image and likeness and that form its knowledge of itself. It says, My ideas tell Me what I AM. I see all the marvellous ways in which I appear to Myself. Here is the beauty, abundance, wholeness, activity, joy that I AM, and there is no other source for any other knowledge or expression apart from Me. Man, My manifestation, is the experience, the evidence, the awareness, of what I, the only I or Ego, AM. Man is what I AM in self-expression. Thus, in acknowledging this one I as the only capacity to know, you can recognise that everything that you humanly may appear to need or desire is really just telling you what you already include and are.

Mrs. Eddy defines man, in part, as "the compound idea of God, including all right ideas."[6] We have looked at some of these ideas, "the thoughts that I think toward you, saith the Lord."[7] It is the sum total of all right ideas that constitute God's knowledge of Himself, and this is His manifestation, or man. All these right ideas make up our practical experience. What makes this the Science of *being*, and not just a philosophy, is found in the degree that we assimilate the divine nature. This is gained by letting these qualities that express God occupy consciousness, and only thus do they transform experience.

The Scientific Yardstick

It is in knowing God, and so finding what man is, that we attain the yardstick that allows us to recognise and reject that which this man is not. In his letter to the Galatians, Paul made a second list of characteristics of which he said, "The works of the flesh are manifest." It includes the thoughts that are selfish, sensual, debased, divisive, and hateful.[8] These thoughts, far from being the offspring of God, are classified as "the children of the wicked one." They are the thoughts of the carnal mind, or "enmity against God," which do not inherit or experience the kingdom of God. They constitute a burlesque of man. The "flesh... manifest" is not the manifestation, or man, of God. It is the consequence of original sin, or the acceptance of an *origin* other than the virgin origin and purity of the divine Mind.

These two lists of thoughts — the fruits of the Spirit and the works of the flesh manifest — do not have equal validity. The first represents the conception, or interpretation, of the divine Principle. The second refers to misconceptions that stem from ignorance of the truth. The first consists of the eternal ideas of the divine Mind. The second refers to beliefs that do not have ultimate reality. Science and Health explains that "from beginning to end, whatever is mortal is composed of material human beliefs and of nothing else."[9] As understanding replaces ignorance, beliefs yield to ideas, the "children of God." But, like East and West, the twain shall never meet.

Watching thought rather than observing physical personality, be it that of others or what we call our own, is both important and practical. It is important because so long as a sense of duality remains, before the pure consciousness of good is found to preclude any other sense of Life, it is necessary to both love the good and reject the evil from thought. In the example of Christ Jesus, he never accepted a thought that did not have its origin in what he called his Father. He referred to this thinking as the Son of God. It was the Christ-consciousness that emanated from universal Mind. In similar manner, he referred to what the world saw of him, as a mortal like any other, as the Son of man. And to make it clear that he did not accept this mortal definition of himself or experience as relating to him, he spoke of "the Son of man which is in heaven."[10] In other words, he was showing that no matter what the physical sense conceived him to be, his conscious identity, the I or Ego, remained with the Father.

An Illusory Ego

It is the whole picture of a mortal ego, and not merely the aspects of it that we find baneful, that is to be rejected as having nothing to do with man. "The ego is not self-existent matter animated by mind, but in itself is mind..."[11] Here the lower case is used in the spelling of ego and mind. It indicates, once again, that the problems of a mortal ego, which remains a misconception of the one and only identity, are not to be solved from within its terms of reference. The mortal ego is a package. This answers the question, How could this happen to me? Or, How could this happen to a good person like A or B? Identification as a mortal opens the door to the general beliefs of mortality, whether we are consciously taking them in or not. The container includes its contents. Exemption from material law lies in finding our immunity from the mortal ego.

Many readers will know the lines from a poem, My Shadow, by Robert Louis Stevenson:

> I have a little shadow that goes in and out with me
> And what can be the use of him is more than I can see.

It is the mortal ego that is the shadow, and though it may be called by the name of Tom, Dick, or Harry, it is no way associated with Me. Moreover, we know that at noon-tide there is no shadow, and man lives as noon-tide glory, neither dawning nor declining.

Thought Constitutes Experience

Watching thought, therefore, is not just important but also practical. Indeed, if it were not so, and if it did not pertain to daily existence where, apparently, we have to respond to the need to eat, sleep, work, find a purpose, and relate to others, this Science would be of little use. It is therefore worth repeating an earlier statement that it is always the sense, or consciousness, of something that is all there is to it. The sense of the storm in the Indian port *was* the storm. There was no storm, however real the physical senses reported it to be, outside the sense of it, and this sense was inherent in the mesmerism, not in reality. To have tried to offset the effects of the storm, when there was no storm in the first place, would have been pointless. The problem was not the storm, but the false sense.

So it is the *sense* with which we do everything that matters. It is not the dish we cook, the bed we make, the clothes we wear, the behaviour of those around us, the home we maintain, that are, in themselves, important, but the quality of thought that constitutes what we are doing. It is this that transforms drudgery into praise, and bathes what we do in the atmosphere of Truth. A friend, suffering from a severe illness, remarked, "It all seems so clear, when I am in your office, but what happens when I return home to the kitchen sink?" The answer was, "Sacred soapsuds!" In other words, it is not what we do, but the spirit, or thought with which we do it, that matters. As an Anglican hymn says:

> who sweeps a room as for Thy laws,
> Makes that and th' action fine.

As the thoughts, or children, of God occupy consciousness, so experience is imbued with the character of its divine source. Jesus did not set out to be a good carpenter, but the altitude from which he lived made him one.

It is what God knows, what is true from the standpoint of Principle, that is our concern, for this knowledge is the true man. The thoughts of God act as a guiding and a shining light. They offset the baneful effects of believing that there is any other source of thought. For example, when

85

the thoughts of lack or sorrow, age or blight, regret or fear, claim a foothold in consciousness, and when we replace these with what is true of Life, from the standpoint of Life itself, this is not just positive, human thinking. It is the conscious, intelligent aligning of thought with the one Mind, the only legitimate thinker. This acts as a power and presence of good in our experience. It immediately begins to outshine the shadows of ignorance with the light of understanding, so that what formerly appeared "through a glass darkly" is seen in God's light. Science, or understanding, does nothing to what is seen; it just removes the dark glass.

A member of my family had put her hip out of joint so that she was only able to walk sideways like a crab. She left the room to call a practitioner, who said, "The only stature is the 'stature of the fullness of Christ.'"[12] Immediately she was upright and returned to the room walking normally. In this case, we see that the patient's belief had no more to do with the real man than a shadow cast on a wall touches the wall. The removal of the belief, or shadow, did not change her but revealed more clearly what she already was.

Nothing true or worthwhile is lost as we yield up the assessment of man as any sort of personal ego, good or bad. The good is enhanced because it is seen as something far bigger than that which is circumscribed by a personal identity. And the bad, being impersonalized, loses its foothold in human character. It is recognised as a false sense, or belief, claiming to be person but not pertaining to him or you. Thus a stature and fullness of character shine through, revealing more clearly the higher nature of man. Truth is less obscured by error.

It is not for nothing that the greatest, most memorable, and distinctive characters in history have combined personal humility with spiritual greatness. Mere personal greatness is ambivalent. It is accompanied by its seamy side. And the picture of personal humility is likewise deceptive. Both personal self-aggrandizement and self-abasement carry the stain of life that is separate from the One. And those who, for the moment, have epitomized the greatest evil and received public acclaim nevertheless, have historically met a fate that, in the language of the Bible, causes people to "narrowly look upon thee... saying, Is this the man that made the earth to tremble, that did shake kingdoms; that made the world as a wilderness... that opened not the house of his prisoners?"[13]

In the long run, evil does not succeed. It appears to repeat itself only so long as we try to deal with its phenomena instead of the false sense itself.

There is only one kind of Life, one kind of man, one kind of experience. What appears as human existence is not an alternative to the divine, but *is* the divine misconceived through the distorting lens of the human mind. The advice above the Delphic oracle, which is also found on temples in the East and should be inscribed in our hearts, is "Know thyself." Know what you are from the standpoint of your Principle; discover what you are in the knowledge of God, and that will, in turn, take care of what you are not. The body, or experience, is always transformed by the renewing of Mind. It is thought that we watch, because it is thought that is true of ourself, for this self-knowledge is the manifestation, or man, of God. In the final analysis, as we saw in the last chapter, man is that which causes his Principle to say THAT I AM, and the substance, life, intelligence, and capacity of this man remain in the Principle that alone knows and constitutes him.

9

Rules and Laws.

There is but one law for all, namely,
that law which governs all laws,
the law of our Creator.
                    Edmund Burke

God is Love, but God is also law.
                    Robert Browning

God's laws, and their intelligent and
harmonious action, constitute his [man's]
individuality in the Science of Soul.
                    Mary Baker Eddy

In the last chapter, we examined two views of man. One was the mortal, which presented man as a human personality consisting of material beliefs. The other referred to man's spiritual individuality — the manifestation of God — as the compound idea of God including all right ideas. In both cases, the definition was in terms of thought, not physique, and the difference lay in the origin of the thinking that constituted the manifestation. We will now look more closely at what is meant by the terms "beliefs" and "ideas" and their relevance to daily living.

In any science, there has to be an unchanging principle as well as a set of concepts, or ideas, that embody this principle. In mathematics, for example, the concept, or idea, that 2+2=4 expresses the principle of mathematics. Because this concept can never deviate from its principle, it is also a rule. A student of mathematics embraces the idea and abides by its rule in solving a problem. The sum is referred to as the "body of knowledge" that expresses its principle.

Spiritual Law Eternal and Universal

The character of an idea, or rule, is that it is eternal and universal. No matter when you were born, or where you live, or even if you do not know anything about the rule, it is always there to recognise and practice. The very nature of an idea is that it is present wherever its principle is, and wherever the mind that knows that principle is to be found.

A friend ordered some carpets for her home. The store told her that these came from China, and that there was generally some discrepancy in the measurements for that reason. Her reply was that mathematics was the same in China as in London, because it expressed the same principle in both places. The carpets arrived and fitted exactly, without a millimeter of error.

Now, just because we are talking about Spiritual Science, the Science of being, it does not mean there can be any departure from the same scientific approach. The only difference between this Science and what is accepted as physical science is that the latter refers to a physical environment and human application, whereas the former operates and is expressed as consciousness. In physical science, the attempt is made to increase and enhance the capacity of a human mind, whereas Spiritual Science demands that the obscuration of this so-called mind, together with its theories, yield to the divine, universal Mind and the ideas that are already expressing it.

The body of knowledge, or Science of being, is the set of

ideas, concepts, or rules that express its divine Principle. In Biblical language, this expression is termed the image and likeness of God. It is the way that Principle is manifest. Some of these ideas, or rules, are joy, abundance, freedom, strength, activity, purpose, and so on. "I know the thoughts that I think toward you, saith the Lord,"[1] and it is these thoughts that constitute and uphold man. They constitute the body, or embodiment, of knowledge that makes up the real man's identity. This body of the infinite is a body of thought or understanding. It is the only body, and is man and the universe. It is the understanding of this one body that appears as the law of restitution to every belief of bodies many.

Ideas, or Rules, Made Practical.

Let us look further at the ideas of God, which are always rules or laws. It may be helpful to take an illustration from a physical science, such as building a bridge. You have to begin with the principle of the relevant science, knowing that the rules that express this principle constitute the appropriate body of knowledge. These rules operate in one way, namely, as consciousness, and it is only as the rules occupy consciousness that the action which follows will be successful. The rules, have, of course, always existed, even before the human perception of them and, if something goes wrong, you get back to the principle and rules. Only in this way can an understanding of the rules dispel the ignorance that caused a mistake, together with the consequence of this ignorance which, in this case, might lead to the collapse of the bridge .

In Spiritual Science the sequence is the same. The rules of this Science are active as ideas. When the ideas of the divine Principle occupy consciousness, they act as guiding laws to experience. In solving a problem, which might appear as lack, loneliness, ill-health, or joblessness, we do not begin with the problem but with the specific idea about which the problem is a misstatement. Lack is not something in its own right but implies ignorance of the plenitude of being. Loneliness is ignorance of completeness, ill-health of wholeness, joblessness of the eternal activity of divine Life. It is always a false sense — and not phenomena — that is dispelled.

No one would deny that, at a certain level, this ignorance does seem palpable and real. But so does the imminent collapse of a bridge which is being built in a way that does not accord with the rules The need is always to get back to what is true from the standpoint of the Principle. You do not try to apply the truth *to* ignorance, but you find that, in understanding what *is* true from a higher standpoint, the ignorance or deflection of this truth disappears in the light of understanding. The right idea, and so the solution, is found wherever its Principle is, and wherever the Mind that *is* that Principle is to be found. The same Mind cannot contain both an understanding and an ignorance of itself. So we read, "It is our ignorance of God, the divine Principle, which produces apparent discord, and the right understanding of Him restores harmony."[2]

The Character of Belief

Ignorance of the principle and its rules does not have the same validity and characteristics as an idea, and so we classify it as a theory or belief. For example, the ignorance that believes 2+2=5, or any number other than 4, is neither eternal nor universal. It is found only where and when the principle is not understood. The moment the rule, or true idea, is understood, the ignorant belief dissolves into nothingness. But the idea must be understood, not just believed. The understanding that 2+2=4 precludes the belief that it is any other number, but merely to learn that it is not 5 produces no such assurance.

This is why we always begin with the principle of a science and the idea that expresses it, and not with the ignorance. When Jesus said, "Ye shall know the truth, and the truth shall make you free,"[3] he made the point that the knowledge of Truth is freedom itself since, in this knowledge, there is no ignorance. Knowing the truth does not have an effect, but *is* the effect of Truth knowing, and this knowledge precludes all unlike itself. He did not say that you have to know the truth *about* a mistake, for this would entail starting with a mistake. Nor did he say that true knowledge would do something *to* a mistake. The implication of his words was simply that, in the presence of Truth, a mistake gives itself up spontaneously. Indeed, from the standpoint of Truth, the Principle, it never was.

Truth is always law. In response to the question, "How would you define Christian Science?," Mrs. Eddy replies, "As the law of God, the law of good, interpreting and demonstrating the divine Principle and rule of universal harmony."[4] When the ideas, laws, rules, of the divine Principle constitute consciousness, man is living as the functioning presence of this Principle, and so as the law of good to his experience.

Beliefs Invalid

The beliefs and theories of the human misconception are always forms of ignorance. The reason that lack and sickness — or any of the other problems of mankind — are classified as beliefs, is that, however real within their own terms of reference, they do not satisfy the criteria of an idea, because they are neither universal nor eternal. Not everyone, everywhere, is sick or lacking at the same time, nor do such beliefs have an unchanging principle. There is no such thing as universal, eternal mumps or bankruptcy.

The beliefs of physique, race, class, upbringing, environment, and the economy likewise cannot satisfy the criteria for being ideas. For example, we all know how medical, economic, social, religious, and other theories change. No one could pretend that they are unchanging laws, and they last only so long as the organizations that support them. It is only if we accept these theories as laws, or true concepts, and then react by fearing or obeying them, that we appear to come under their jurisdiction. Only the ideas of God satisfy the criteria of being universal, self-existent, and independent of human opinion, sanction, or conditions.

Let us consider the example of economics. This is not a science, but its theories express the current opinions of economists. However far they stretch, they do not reach a conclusion. To accept the theories regarding recession, market forces, or the distribution of scarce resources as true, and then to adjust one's life-style to them, is not much more sensible than trying to adjust the progress of a train in order to conform to the apparently converging railway lines in the distance. The factors that govern the human economy are mental and moral. It is not difficult to see the blight that ensues from greed, selfishness, or fear, but the opposite ideas of God, embraced as consciousness, and so rules by which we abide, offset these effects. Throughout history, there have been examples of those who have understood something of these rules and who have been sustained, in times of dearth, by a higher law. The Bible abounds in examples of those who have understood the sustaining law of Truth. That same law has been proved in the modern concentration camps and when people have been confronted by privation elsewhere.

Beliefs Not Laws

We should understand that, just as Truth is law, so ignorance of Truth is an outlaw, however it may masquerade as legality. It would seem that there are many beliefs, or aspects of ignorance, that constitute what is called mortal (or dead) existence. What one consciously misconceives of oneself, as a person, is only a fraction of what is floating around in the general atmosphere of the human mind. This is why our exemption from the lawlessness of ignorance lies in the total release of the personal definition of oneself as a little mortal ego, in the awareness of man's true identity as Principle in self-expression. The fruits of the Spirit are rules, and "against such there is no law."

But how does this work in practice? The whole point is that, because we are watching only thought and its origin, rather than material phenomena, this approach is entirely practical. In fact, we are never trying to put right the storm in the Indian port. We are exchanging, within our own consciousness, a material for a spiritual *view* of the one and only situation. Then, because the former does not exist outside the sense of it, the removal of this *sense* appears as the situation conforming to a higher law.

Discovering a New Identity

A man was sent to my office. He was not interested in coming but did so to please the only member of his family with whom he was still in touch. This visitor presented a sorry picture. Dishevelled, unshaven, possessing only one dirty suit of clothes, jobless, drinking heavily, disowned by his family, and wanted on charges by the police of three countries. We spoke in simple terms of a higher identity and selfhood than the unsatisfactory one that he was presenting, and that, since this identity was a law, he could not escape finding it.

A new sense of identity began to dawn, almost in spite of himself. That same day he got a Christmas job in a big store. The next day, during the lunch hour, he ran into his father, who was shopping there. His father apparently recognised some change, for he bought his son new clothes and invited him to spend Christmas with the family. When he came for a second interview in the New Year, he was a changed man: clean, reconciled to his family, upright, free of drink, and with a new purpose in life. Shortly after this, the police in all three countries dropped their charges against him; he was offered a farm manager's job in another country, and is now happy, successful, and married, with a family.

Universal Living

What was the law in this case? Simply that his higher identity was the truth, and the picture presented was the aberration. His true identity, being composed of universal rules, or ideas, had to be recognised universally, for it was only ignorance that was localized and divisive. This appeared as a new recognition by the father and his family, his new employer, and also the police for, in their case, the charges could only have been preferred against the human misconception of man, and never against the manifestation of God. Disassociated from this ignorant misconception, he was disassociated from its penalty. He had risen to the level where "all things work together for good to them that love God."

When the ideas of God, instead of the beliefs of the human mind, are present as consciousness, experience inevitably enters new dimensions. We begin to live universally instead of personally. We begin to experience what it means to "be absent from the body, and to be present with the Lord."[5] A personal ego, or little "i", always thinks and speaks in localized, limited, fragmentary, and divisive tones. It says "i" am frustrated, sick, sad, afraid, unemployed, struggling and getting nowhere." Such statements do not express law, and it is not just what this personal ego says, but its right to say anything at all, that is disputed. To let this little "i" speak or to admit what it says into consciousness, gives it the only power it could seem to have. The ideas of God are always expressed from the standpoint of the divine I, or Ego. They are always infinite, eternal, universal concepts such as, "I am freedom, harmony, boundless bliss, joy, wholeness." These are laws.

The Daily Practice.

Mrs. Eddy asks, "How are veritable ideas to be distinguished from illusions?" And her answer is, "By learning the origin of each. Ideas are emanations from the divine Mind. Thoughts, proceeding from the brain or from matter, are offshoots of mortal mind; they are mortal material beliefs."[6] The distinction between ideas and beliefs is not gained by asking "What did he, or she, or they, or even the little "i" say or do, but did I, the only I, say it, do, know, or experience it?" And the practical import of this is that when some statement or picture does not gain lodgement as consciousness, it finds itself barred from experience. This distinction is the daily practice of this Science.

A woman had an irate telephone conversation with her grown daughter late one evening. She relayed this in some detail, and with considerable indignity, to a friend who was a practitioner. He reminded her that she owned a book (the Bible) in which it says that our conversation is made in heaven. She was asked whether this was a heavenly conversation. When she repeated the unjust things that had been said to her, she was asked whether these were true from the standpoint of divine Love. She was told to ask herself whether I, Truth, had said such things about Myself, or whether I, Love, could do such things to Myself, and then to allow only what was true and lovely from the standpoint of the divine Mind to abide in thought. Shortly after, the daughter called back and apologized — something she had never been known to do before.

Living as the law of Principle in operation does not mean using this Principle to patch up a mistaken view of the universe. The Highway Code is not designed to patch up the result of accidents but to ensure that driving takes place according to the rules which themselves preempt accidents. In this way, experience remains harmonious and intact. Likewise, adherence to the rules and laws of God in every aspect of daily life — and so the apprehension of the divine nature and character — exempts experience from discord. This implies more than just human goodness; it involves existence from a new standpoint. As the Psalmist wrote, "Open thou mine eyes, that I may behold wondrous things out of thy law."[7]

The rules or laws that constitute the Science of being are as exact and undeviating as those that concern any discipline of physical science. Their demands are moral and spiritual. They entail the assimilation of the divine character. They permit no opposite and brook no alternative, and man's identification with them is inescapable. And why should one wish it otherwise, when there is nothing to lose but ignorance of the eternal laws, or ideas, of good?

The mathematician's practice is inescapable from the principle of his practice. The metaphysician's practice is likewise inseparable from its Principle. The only difference is that, in the first case, the mathematician regards himself as a personal practitioner. In Science, Principle constitutes its own practice, with no person in the way. Man then lives as this Principle in self-expression as laws, rules, and ideas.

10

Mediation and Atonement

By whatever name you call me,
it is I who will answer.

Krishna

The view of the scientific I explains God and man in new terms and reveals their oneness. It has also shown that everything is dealt with at the point of consciousness, and that there is nothing outside consciousness to be reached or to require a mediator. In fact to speak of the relationship *between* God and man is inaccurate since the infinite, indivisible One admits nothing between itself. Now let us look from the same scientific viewpoint at some of the religious and secular fruits of believing in a separation between God and man, or cause and effect. This inevitably includes an examination of some of the most cherished religious opinions.

One Requires No Mediator

The concepts of mediation and intercession are common to most, if not all, religions. Yet, in no place is the scientific viewpoint more blurred than in those concepts. If the approach is one of a limited, human personality trying to attain something infinitely greater than itself, then the gap between promise and fulfillment seems to require something or someone to bridge it. This role has been traditionally filled by the intercession of priesthood, and thus by the assumption that there are those who, by some dispensation, know more then we do and, so to speak, have the ear of God. The veil of the temple, in Jewish theology, signified the belief that the face of God was hidden from the ordinary mortal. Only those with special qualifications could penetrate beyond the veil.

Accompanying this belief in a personal mediator are two further beliefs. The first is that, balancing some personal ability to reach up to God, or reality, is the attribution to God of near-human characteristics which, in turn, allow God to hear and come down to human needs. This is the inevitable result of personalizing our concept of God and of man. The second habit of thought is belief in the efficacy of sacrifice in order to propitiate and appease something beyond man. The pagan sacrifice of animals has yielded to a less physical sense whereby the human has to give up something cherished in order to become worthy of the divine. This whole approach, however, retains the basic premise of something that is, at present, fragmentary and unworthy, attaining, by some means or another, the worthiness and wholeness that, instinctively, are felt to be true and to be man's heritage.

A further result of the scenario which arises from this basic premise is that prayer tends to be restricted to supplication. This presupposes a God who can be induced to come down and respond to localized, finite situations. It suggests that pure, infinite Mind can take cognizance of things that are foreign to its own nature and thereby depart from its own character. The reductio ad absurdum of this concept is found in battle, when both sides pray to the same God for victory over their enemies.

None of the above disregards the value of the thought behind intercession and supplication. Indeed, such prayer is often the highest human expression of love and compassion for those in need. It expresses the humility that turns to a higher power when the human has reached its frontiers of capability. But such prayer is a step towards something higher, for it is in finding our true and present relation to God, rather than in expecting God to relate to personal situations, that our human needs appear as being met. The whole concept of a need for something between God and mortal man is based on the belief that the latter cannot fulfill divine demands without help, nor find his oneness with a perfect God. As man recognises a higher identity, he finds this oneness.

The command, "Put off thy shoes,"[1] which came to Moses as he stood before the burning bush, expresses the real need, which is to abandon the premise that man ever stood alone separate from God. Then, in this higher understanding, the prayer of supplication gives place to a recognition and awareness of present perfection. In the acknowledgement of man's oneness with all good, which already exists, a sense of need is then transmuted by the alchemy of spirituality into the consciousness of possession. This is the way of devotion and of spiritual understanding.

I recall an incident early in my time with industry. It appeared that the salary at which I had started was totally inadequate for my basic needs, let alone commensurate with the experience that I had had in former work. As I walked across a London park to work, I found myself becoming conscious of the abundance I saw all around me — the grass, the leaves on the trees, the sunlight, and so on. I found that my financial worries were dropping away in the awareness of abundance. When I reached the office, I was informed that my manager wished to see me, and I found that his reason for doing so was to offer me a rise in salary.

A New Rationality

Spiritual rationality and free thought are today questioning this whole attitude towards mediation, propitiation, and prayer. The basic assumption, in both religious and secular fields, that any group of persons can discharge responsibilities on another's behalf, is being challenged. The tendency on the part of those who, intellectually, feel they have sorted out their human lives may be to hand over the "unseen" side to others. This smacks of ignorance and, sometimes, of hedging one's bets. "I know my business, but I don't know about God, so I go to a priest." The concept of a big God and little man is yielding to an instinctive, and now often expressed, feeling that God is much closer than theology has suggested. And the whole idea of approaching God with a "shopping list" of human requirements, or requests to put right the mess that mankind has made, seems faintly immoral. It taints our view of both God and man.

Again, this does not decry any turning to God in prayer, but this turning has to be, so to speak, on bended knee. It has to express a genuine desire to let the divine will be apparent. It knows that "every good gift... cometh down from the Father of lights,"[2] but also recognizes that these gifts are qualities of thought, not things as things. Solomon found that when he prayed for an understanding heart, all the other things of human affluence and greatness were thrown in. We must love Truth for Truth's sake. What is immoral is the attitude that we can do as we want and then ask God to fix up the mess we have made, or just have good things without the God who supplies them. The irresponsible man cannot help being immoral. The evidence that the religious tendency has its counterpart in secular affairs, for it is the same state of thought, is dealt with in the chapter, "The Medium and the Message."

No Fallen Man

If these former concepts are yielding, what takes their place? The misconceptions of atonement and prayer arise from the basic premise that man, as idea, has a separate life and mind from God, or Principle. The true conception has to begin from the basis of the indissoluble relationship of this Principle and its idea. "The vail that is spread over all nations"[3] is not a veil between one group of persons and another, but the fundamental error that would shut experience out of natural good and worthiness. The belief that there has ever been an initial fall from grace by man, and so a subsequent need for redemption, is obsolete. It is an assumption that is derived only from the testimony of the physical senses, which always present an inverted view of that which is unfallen. The release of the false assumption then releases the whole problem of inequity between God and man, which has perplexed believers and theologians throughout the ages.

An interesting experience, which illustrates this, occurred when I was in the Army in Kenya. A district officer had decided on some forest clearance, but he was approached by the local witch doctor who said that, if this work went ahead, a certain spirit, who inhabited a nearby tree, would be offended, and great trouble would come upon the tribe. The district officer did not accept this, and so the work proceeded. Shortly after, the witch doctor came to him and said that the tree in question had fallen to the ground, and that the tribesmen were standing around it, wondering what was going to happen.

The district officer set off to see the situation for himself, but what he found was not what he expected. Because of his background — the mental framework within which his own experience had taken place — he indeed saw the tribe looking at the tree on the ground, but he saw it still standing upright. It was a case of mass mesmerism. He then said to the witch doctor, "I see what you have done, but you are a very clever man, and you are going to make that tree come upright again." So, while he continued to see the tree upright, he watched the tribesmen follow it with their eyes from the fallen to the upright position.

The lesson is obvious in its wider application. Just as the sense of the storm at the Indian port *was* the storm, and just as the sense of a fallen tree *was* the fallen tree, might we not consider that the sense, or interpretation, of man as a fallen, sinning, sick, and dying mortal is all there is to that picture? Which was of the greater help to the African tribesmen? A human mediator who would restore a fallen tree, or the removal of mesmerism in the understanding that the tree had never fallen? And, if the latter, would not the same choice be valid between an intercessory, acting on behalf of a fallen man, and a Saviour, in the form of understanding, who would point out that man was never other than upright? This ties in with an earlier quotation which reads, "Jesus beheld in Science the perfect man, who appeared to him where sinning mortal man appears to mortals. In this perfect man the Saviour saw God's own likeness, and this correct view of man healed the sick."[4] This is a practical example of the Saviour, Immanuel or God with us, for in the conscious presence of Truth, the mistake disappears.

A Fresh Start

The release that comes in Science from the understanding that Principle and its idea, or man, is one, is beyond words. No longer is the starting point that of something to be put right. Instead, it is the innate rightness of being when seen and interpreted from the standpoint of its divine Principle. Then, what appear, to another standpoint of perception, as a material universe and a sinning mortal man are recognized, not as an alternative to the pure, blameless, and eternal nature of being, but as just a mis-conception of it. And, since that misconception could arise only from a suppositional standpoint outside the infinite, it has to be nothing but mesmerism or myth.

What are the results of basing one's appreciation of mediation, sacrifice, and prayer on the eternal oneness, wholeness, and perfection of being, as seen through the lens of the divine Mind, instead of accepting the interpretation of the physical senses, or the carnal mind?

The first is that the belief in mediumship, or mediation, is dropped and, with it, the thought that any person can discharge the responsibilities of another. There can be no intercession, or inter-communion, between ignorance and understanding, person and Principle, matter and Spirit, the human and the divine, or, between nothing and something. That which is already and eternally one does not have to be made one, but precludes that which does not conform to itself. In dropping the belief in a medium, the belief that the onus for perfection is on the human is also dropped. Intercession no longer means vicarious salvation but the individual capacity to shed all belief that being is divided into myriads of personal minds and lives. Ignorance does not attain understanding but yields to it. "The divine understanding reigns, is *all*, and there is no other consciousness."[5]

The second result is that sacrificial atonement gives place to living, in the detail of daily life, man's at-one-ment with his Principle, God. "Atonement is the exemplification of man's unity with God, whereby man reflects divine Truth, Life, and Love."[6] Elsewhere, Mrs. Eddy writes, "To live so as to keep human consciousness in constant relation with the divine, the spiritual, and the eternal, is to individualize infinite power; and this is Christian Science."[7] This consciousness of everything from the standpoint of the divine, and living in accord with it, makes sacred (the real meaning of "sacrifice") all that we do. All that is given up is a false, limited sense for the true *sense* of being and, in dropping that false sense, the subsidiary errors that it includes are dropped with it. The divine nature, thus recognised and lived, has no need to propitiate itself.

The third result is that prayer moves from a mode of supplication to a way of life. It is a constant affirmation of and rejoicing in what is true; it is disassociation from all that is not true; it is the yielding of thought, will, feeling, and interpretation to God. In this way do we obey the commandment to love God with all our heart, and soul, and mind — all our affection, feeling, and knowing. It is prayer when the voice of God is our voice; the vision of God is our vision; the ears of God are our ears; and the activity of God is our activity. How, otherwise, do we fulfill the command, "Be ye therefore perfect, even as your Father which is in heaven is perfect?"[8] In this oneness of being, prayer becomes a paeon of praise and gratitude; beliefs have yielded to understanding; salvation ceases to be a goal, because it is the release from all identity with that which appears to be in need of saving from sickness, sin, and death. In that consciousness which is in constant relation to the Father, there is no possibility of a departure from perfection, so no need for taking measures to reach perfection. The veil is lifted, and man is found no more in need of saving but already and eternally saved.

Truth Heals.

A woman psychiatrist, accompanied by her husband, came to my office to discuss some questions concerning Christian Science. After a pleasant conversation she said, "I'm sure my husband would like a word with you." He did not seem to have any questions, but he did say that this sort of subject did not have much interest for him. However, he had a problem. For a long time the fingers on one hand had been rigid, and he could not open them. Almost without realizing it, I just said, "But Love is expansive. It never contracts." Two days later, the lady called to say that her marriage which, on the day she came, had been at its lowest ebb, had suddenly become as happy as it had ever been. Then she said again, "My husband would like a word with you." He said that, the same evening, his fingers had opened, and his hand was normal. The understanding of the true nature of Love had been appreciable at each level of his experience.

The point can be made here that this episode did not in fact involve one person intervening on behalf of another, even though this might have been how it seemed. In explaining what happened, it may be useful to return to the analogy of the window panes to which reference was made earlier. It was seen that the pane had no inherent light, nor was the sunlight that shone through confined to it. The light is always the indivisible light of the sun, and it shines brightest through the pane that is clearest. It is shed on all that is within its range. Window pane "A" does not seek light from window pane "B." In the practice of Science, it is never a question of some person interceding on behalf of another or even directing healing thoughts at another. It is in the degree that any sense of a personal mind or capacity gets out of the way that the light of understanding shines through and dissolves ignorance. A single statement of Truth, just because it is true, has the might of omnipotence behind it. Truth, not person, heals.

Inevitably this all leads to a new view of the role and mission of Christ Jesus as the Way-shower in Christian thinking. The questioning of some of the time-honoured views on this subject is already widespread. But such questioning can lead only to an enhanced view of one who will always stand pre-eminent as the Master to those who follow his precepts, and the Way to those who identify with what he taught. Nothing could ever denigrate the enormity of his life and works nor the purpose of his mission, which he expressed in his own words, "I am come that they might have life, and that they might have it more abundantly."[9] A deeper treatment of the Saviour and his mission follows in the chapter which has these words as its title.

11

The Mission of the Saviour

*You are under the power of no other
enemy, are held in no other captivity,
and want no other deliverance, but from
the power of your own earthly self.
This is the murderer of the divine Life
within you. It is your own Cain
that murders your own Abel.*

William Law

*He [the Christ] is our peace, who hath
made both one, and hath broken down
the middle wall of partition between us.*

Ephesians

The Moral Law

The great contribution of Jewish thought, expressed in the
Old Testament of the Bible, was the portrayal of a moral
and righteous God, who, in turn, demanded obedience to
an undeviating, if stern and exacting, moral law. The Ten
Commandments, given to Moses and expanded into rules
that based the minutiae of daily existence on this law, are
scarcely disputed as codes of behaviour by any of the
great religions. However, Eastern thought, with its metaphysical standpoint, has dwelt more obviously with higher levels of consciousness as steps towards ultimate reality than with a humanly moral law. In the East the moral
law is more implicit, and the language tends to be more
that of light and darkness, understanding and ignorance,
reality and the dream, than that of standards of daily
behaviour.

The moral law, however imperfectly observed, has acted widely as some brake on physical excess and has developed a keener ability to distinguish between right and wrong. So much is this so that some of the worst acts by this century's tyrants have had to be proclaimed and justified in the name of good and right. The limitation, however, is that unless the moral code is spiritually, rather than personally, based, it is liable to display the general duality of the human mind. This means that the moral quality appears equally likely to have an immoral opposite. Temperance and excess, patience and impatience, honesty and dishonesty, seem to be in harness, and the gap between humanity's best efforts and its achievements remains.

The Higher Law

The advent of Christ Jesus in the Western world, and the teachings that are expressed in the New Testament, did not put aside but enhanced the moral law by setting it on a spiritual basis and a religion of Love. He said that he had come to fulfill, but not destroy, the law that he, like other Jews, had been educated to observe. But by basing the provisions of the Commandments on spiritual law, he was lifting their import to a level where they were universally true, thus not only fulfilling Mosaic law but complementing the metaphysical teaching of other religions. Thus the moral law is seen to be not just a human code but actual spiritual law shining through the belief that it is merely human.

Jesus clarified the new, spiritual sense of the law by contrasting it with the old. In just this way we can see how the scientific viewpoint on the Ten Commandments[1] changes the "shalt not" to "canst not."

The First and Second Commandments say, "Thou shalt

have no other gods before me" and "Thou shalt not make unto thee any graven image," but "I" say unto you that he who knows that I AM the Lord cannot help having no other gods, no other sense of life, truth, or substance but ME. Thus, the making of images and similitudes, by ascribing anything of truth and substance to the external world of appearances, is precluded. Objectification becomes impossible.

The Third Commandment says that thou shalt not take the name of the Lord in vain, but "I" say that this is impossible when it is learned that there is no other standpoint, no other capacity, but the Lord in the first place.

The Fourth Commandment reminds us to "remember the sabbath day, to keep it holy." This day is the consciousness that sees everything that is made and knows it to be very good. So "I" say that the Mind that I AM cannot be conscious of anything but the wholeness, completeness, and goodness of My own being.

The Fifth Commandment says, "Honour thy father and thy mother," but "I" say unto you that the one Parent has to be acknowledged as the source and origin of all instead of any human parentage.

The Sixth Commandment says, "Thou shalt not kill," but "I" say unto you that the one who understands infinite Life cannot kill by holding a mortal, or dead, concept of anyone or anything.

The Seventh Commandment says, "Thou shalt not commit adultery," but "I" say unto you that the consciousness of Mind could not be adulterated by any element foreign to itself.

The Eighth and Tenth Commandments say "Thou shalt

not steal" or "covet" thy neighbour's possessions, but "I" say unto you that he who understands the subjective nature of being, in which the right idea about everything is already included in his own self-completeness, could not possibly covet or steal.

The Ninth Commandment says, "Thou shalt not bear false witness against thy neighbour," but "I" say unto you that knowing the indivisibility of being, one finds it impossible to bear false witness against another without accepting this falsity for oneself.

The Apostle John wrote, "Whosoever is born of God doth not commit sin; for his seed remaineth in him: and he cannot sin, because he is born of God."[2] Thought that has its origin in and emanates from the divine Mind cannot depart from the source and nature of its Principle.

Jesus and the Christ

It was because the detail of his life was subject to and characterized by his spiritual source that Jesus was able to say, "I am from above," even while the mortal sense of him, held by those around him, could see only a son of man like themselves. The onlookers based their assessment on physicality, so that even their finest human concept was limited to some extent. His basis was spiritual, and throughout his career he demonstrated freedom from the physical, material assessment of any situation, and this enabled him to do the great works. It was always the Christ-consciousness — his identity as the Son, or self-expression of Truth — that constituted what he knew of himself or others, and never what the human perception reckoned him to be. And it was the understanding of what was spiritually true, when limited perception was presenting lack, sickness, fear, sin, and the grave, that saved, redeemed, and healed. Science and Health explains that "the divinity of the Christ was made manifest in the humanity of Jesus."[3]

The problems and disputes about his career and mission have always arisen when people have tried to personalize, and so restrict, their import. The theology that sees "the only begotten Son" as person, and thus equates the Christ with a personal Saviour, has inevitably lost sight of much that he said about himself. This has relegated the practical meaning of all he was teaching and proving to personality and a period in time. It has led to an acceptance that his works were a special dispensation rather than an expression of an eternal law. Thus, the promise that all who believed on him should do the same works has been largely ignored or forgotten. The great composer, Brahms, referred to this promise as follows: "According to Jesus' own words, He was in that case not the great exception, but the great example for us to emulate." Unless we understand that, behind the miracles of physical healing, lay an ever-operative and demonstrable Science, the import of his mission is largely hidden. It has also confined the Saviour to a particular period and creed, thus making his mission unpalatable to a large portion of mankind because it limits his message to a particular culture or set of beliefs. The Principle that he taught and practiced has been obscured by thought that buries its sense of the truth in the sepulchre of personality. Yet Truth must be universal and incorporeal, if it is to be true at all. It was the scientific I, not person, that healed the blind man 2,000 years ago and heals today.

It is possible to find in the Gospels, not just a Christian Messiah but a universal saving Principle that transcends time and creed. That Jesus himself saw this is found in his rejection of any attempt by others to personalize good ("Why callest thou me good? there is none good but...

God").[4] It also impelled his recognition that if he, as a person, was not taken away from their sight, the Spirit of Truth, which he called the Comforter, could not appear. As the Way-shower, he was the exemplar but not the exception. He taught the way of holiness. He gave the required standards for this way of living in his great Sermon on the Mount, which was certainly the fulfillment of Mosaic law. He refuted the suggestion that his teaching and practice were the result of any personal relationship with the Father by such statements as, "He that believeth on me, the works that I do shall he do also." And he explained that the reason it was possible to do the works, and even greater ones, was because "I go unto my Father"[5] — because the I, or Ego, was "absent from the body... and present with the Lord." Was this not an indication of the universal and eternal nature of the truth ?

Jesus showed, as it is related in the account of his conversation with Nicodemus, that to let the I go to the Father meant being born again.[6] At first, this seemed hard for Nicodemus, who was a literal-minded man, to understand. But then Jesus explained that he was referring to the source where thought, not physique, was born, and the words he used were, "That which is born of the flesh is flesh, and that which is born of the Spirit is spirit." What mattered was the origin of thought. The new birth that was the prerequisite for new experience was a 180 degree turnaround in thinking so that, like Jesus, his followers could say "I am from above." This, indeed, was true regeneration, for it implied a new origin for the generation of thought. It was also true repentance, a word that actually means "turning round." Thus, the Christian demand for both regeneration and repentance is not ignored but given a spiritual dimension. This new birth, the birth of a new view and experience, can begin now and can be the experience of everyone.

True Sacrifice

How, then, is the immense sacrifice that was made by Christ Jesus to be regarded? Was it just that unimaginable demonstration of love that took place on Calvary, the fulfillment of prophecy, and the expiation for others' sins; or was it something even more wonderful and lasting? Here it is useful to make the distinction between the Christ, or Christ-consciousness, that was and is the Son of God, and Jesus, as the son of man. The former is the Truth that is one with God, as when Jesus said, "I am the way, the truth, and the life,"[7] whereas the latter is the man, who more than any other, taught and exemplified this Truth. The Christ is divine; Jesus was the human man. It is a distinction that he himself made constantly. Christ Jesus meant Jesus, the God-like man.

Did not the real sacrifice that he made, and the one he enjoined his followers to accept, lie in his willingness to "give all for Christ" — to give up all identity with a life, mind, purpose, will, or capacity separate from his Principle, God? The sacrifice or making sacred, as the word implies, was the abandonment of all that would hide his real self, the I AM. The crown that was his reward was the disappearance of the human concept of man before the presence of the divine, the son of man before the Son of God. In this disappearance, the role of a mediator, or intercessor, who would atone for the sins of others, yields to the realization of man's oneness with God — his at-one-ment with his divine Principle.

Science and Health summarizes the difference between the Christ and the human exemplar as follows:

> CHRIST. The divine manifestation of God, which comes to the flesh to destroy incarnate error.[8]

114

> JESUS. The highest human corporeal concept of
> the divine idea, rebuking and destroying error
> and bringing to light man's immortality.[9]

It is the Christ which is "the same yesterday, and today, and forever," and which is the Truth to be embodied and lived, and not just followed. It is the Christ which is the Messiah, Saviour, and Redeemer, and which fulfills the prophecy, "His name shall be called Immanuel, or God with us." God with us means Truth with us, Life with us, Love with us, as our thought and action, and when God is with us in this way, the opposite of God called error, mortality, and hate are not with us. In this presence of God with us, there need be, and can be, no medium between God and man, Principle and idea. The Christ is God with us — not person on behalf of us. But though we are speaking of a Principle, Love, and not person, the practical function of the Christ is always to save, comfort, heal, and redeem. It is the Shepherd that seeks out and leads his flock; the Way of Life that is wholeness now; the Rock of Truth on which to stand, and so ever-present and ever-operative.

Individual Responsibility

Jesus demonstrated the Way but did not do our work for us. No principle can come down to a level that does not represent it correctly, nor could a principle propitiate anything higher than itself. And person, however good, cannot do this either. The saving Principle permits no sense of anything but the Truth. It does not take cognizance of error but effaces it. It forgives sin or any deviation from itself by destroying its possibility, since the true sense of Life precludes a false sense. In laying down all identity with anything less than the divine, we also lay down all that can sin, be sick, deserve punishment, and be destroyed.

The real import of Jesus' sublime career lies in the fact that he showed mortals how to drop identity with the mortal, and thus find the Life that is God to be the only Life, and so exempt from sin, sickness, and death. When these are destroyed in consciousness, they cease to exist. To give all for Christ is the true sense of forgiveness — a word which means to "give something for." It is clear that the body does not sin, and the impulsion to do so comes neither from God nor body but from what St. Paul calls the carnal mind. And if the influence of this so-called mind is removed by the presence of the divine Mind, is not man already saved? What is there left to be punished or redeemed?

To be released from the fetters of belief in a life that is less than, or separate from, the divine, and to be shown how everyone of whatever background, age, class, nation, and of whatever mortal history, can partake of the divine Life, restores man to his primitive and only real status as the Son of God. In this identity as the presence of infinite good, as the operation of Principle in self-expression and of divine Love in self-fulfillment, man does not need to be saved, for he is, literally, the experience of salvation. The door is open for everyone to accept what Christ Jesus taught, to find that this one Life or consciousness is the actual Life or consciousness of man, that has never fallen from perfection and so does not have to be redeemed; that has never entered the mortal misconception of it, so does not have to be healed; that is neither buried nor resurrected from material conditions but is exempt from all unlike God.

In laying down all for Christ by dropping a false sense of identity, we lay down all that can sin, suffer, be sick, threatened, limited, or die. Christ Jesus pointed the way; the Comforter is the understanding of how this is done. Is this not a reason for untold gratitude and for practical living rather than commemoration ? How else does one discharge the debt to the Teacher than by practicing what is taught ?

12

The Medium and the Message

It is easy to see that a greater self-reliance, a new respect for the divinity in man, must work a revolution in all the offices and relations of man; in their religion, in their education, in their pursuits, their modes of living. Discontent is the want of self-reliance. Nothing can bring you peace but yourself.
Emerson

The link between a change in religious concepts and new expressions of science, social behaviour, and art has been mentioned. The viewpoint determines the whole view, and not just a part of it. Thus the belief in a medium, in the religious sense, impacts on the use of media in other fields.

States of thought tend to straddle the boundary between the religious and the secular. The acceptance of the need for a personal or material medium in order to reach and enjoy some truth, or promulgate some idea, is endemic to human experience. It is self-evident that people are conditioned to regard virtually every aspect of their experience as coming from something or someone outside of themselves. I AM – yes, but only because of this or that. Health is conditional on external factors and, if lost, is hopefully redeemed through the medium of materia medica. Supply and activity are subject to personal effort and also the sanction of a bank or an employer. Welfare hinges on government hand-outs; happiness is contingent on

118

other persons or propitious circumstances; even the environment (a word meaning "that which surrounds us") is apparently subject to conditions outside our control. And none of this is surprising, for the view of man, seen through the lens of restricted awareness, presents him as an isolated fragment of existence, tossed to and fro by events and dependent upon other, similar fragments for his well-being.

Derived Means Deprived

The acceptance of the view of existence as derived from the external leads to a number of consequences. The first is that the same factors that determine what is derived can, in a moment, change and become the very means by which man is deprived. An example would be the collapse of the stock market, so that the medium for former supply becomes the means by which that supply is lost. Or the failure of a business, which at one moment had been the source of rightful activity and suddenly becomes the reason for unemployment. In short, nothing that is deemed to be derived can escape the liability of being deprived. The view of man as an incomplete mortal places him at the sport of circumstances. What the world gives, the world has a habit of taking away.

The second consequence is that people are taught to look everywhere but within their own consciousness for the solution to their problems. They seek to correct the phenomena of the view instead of the mental standpoint of perception. A supreme example in recent years is the growth of the welfare state or dependent society. There has arisen a situation where the expectancy of the means to live and prosper is turned from individual self-reliance to the government as the source of supply. While no one should argue against a safety net for those who have some temporary need they cannot meet, the spread of benefits to those who do not need them, and the long-term abdication of an individual's self-reliance, and so the erosion of his self-respect, can only be harmful. It leads to a culture where belief in rights is unmatched by an understanding of responsibilities; an acceptance of something for nothing, and so a loss of values; and the desire to assuage material desires by reliance on the external, irrespective of any moral or spiritual dimension. It encourages the acceptance that a group of persons, called a government, knows better what is good for the individual than he does himself. It then identifies this same government as something to blame if the individual is not satisfied, as inevitably will be the case.

A third consequence of believing in a "derived existence" is that the medium itself becomes increasingly ineffective. At one level we can see how a drug fails to satisfy. A condition that needs one grain to alleviate it soon needs more. An exploration into some new sensual experience leads to the desire to do it again and again. The essence of any addiction is that the outward solution never accomplishes what it promises. At another level, we see that the medium cannot deliver. An example is the way in which government departments become top-heavy, show decreasing competence, and often collapse. Why is it, for instance, that the administration of a great city can become bankrupt? Why does crime escalate, despite the constant resources that are put into fighting it? Why do the colossal sums spent on education and health produce diminishing returns? Of course, there are many learned explanations offered by economists, sociologists, and the like, but these beg the main question. They still represent the attempt to analyse and solve problems from within the parameters of the problem, and this never works. To find a valid solution to these social problems, and a satisfactory way of meeting legitimate needs, an entirely fresh approach is required.

The Impulsion of Ideas

The theme that everything comes to us at the point of consciousness and that we live in a universe of consciousness has been reiterated in this book. "Great men," wrote Emerson, "are they who see that spiritual is stronger than any material force; that thoughts rule the world." The launching pad for progress in any sphere, religious or secular, is an idea. It is ideas that have consequences. It is because "thinking makes it so" that the thought, or concept, of something is not only the impulsion, but also the experience, of something. Webster defines the word "idea" as "the immediate object of understanding," and the word "immediate" means "without a medium." In a universe of consciousness, there can be no medium between Mind and the thoughts, or ideas, it is thinking. Hence "for God to know is to be." Knowing and being are two aspects of the same consciousness. It is only the educated reluctance to accept this knowing as practical and concrete being that leads to the demand that the required concrete must take material form. The more it is understood that the idea of something is the actual substance of that thing, and that substance is not in the "appearance," the more the necessity for a medium will inevitably, though incidentally, recede. Ideas can be distorted, in more or less degree, only by the medium through which they are expressed.

Throughout history, all religious, social, political, and other reforms or innovations have begun with an idea, a vision. A former Member of the British Parliament, W.J. Brown, describes graphically the sequence that ensues in an article entitled "Imprisoned Ideas." He shows that the pure vision of the discoverer is, to some extent, clouded by the imperfect apprehension of the immediate disciples who, in turn, feel the need for some organization to protect and foster the initial vision. With successive generations, however, it is the organization, or medium, rather than the idea that grows in importance in the eyes of those who serve it. There is thus an evident take-over by the "priests of the organization" from "the servants of the Spirit." The organization then, instead of serving the idea behind it — an idea that is to be lived and practiced — increases to the point that the idea is forgotten. Dogma replaces inspiration, formalism takes over from spontaneity, and the meaning is swaddled in the red tape of bureaucracy.

Disenchantment with Organizational Claims

It is only then, at the lowest point, that the "remnant" breaks loose from the organizational fetters and starts again. The monks at St. Mary's York , for example, sickened by the materialism and self-indulgence of a top-heavy and corrupt priesthood, left York to found Fountains Abbey, where they could return to true values. And, in secular affairs, the membership of Greenpeace in Britain exceeds that of all three main political parties together. As a state of thought, the contemporary desire to opt out, even though often negative and without any ideal behind it, reflects the disenchantment that has led before to the cry "A plague on both your houses." It is not without significance that, in Bible history, the size of the tabernacle which, under the prophets, was small and mobile, increased in the proportion that central authority grew as a result of the demand of the people to "make us a king to judge us like all the nations."[1] It is, indeed, the desire for a king, a priest, a government, or a boss of any kind to do our thinking for us that has been, historically, as disastrous as hard to resist. What is certain is that a king who gives us all we want will assuredly take from us all we have .

Returning to the question of government institutions, no

one could dispute the desirability of education, health, law, and order. But what happens, time and again, is that the idea becomes swamped in the effort to organize and institutionalise it in order to put it into effect. While some form of organization may be temporarily useful, it is only by keeping the idea behind it paramount in thought that the organization will remain on tap, not on top. But the moment the medium takes precedence over the idea, or the continuity of the organization is regarded as something in its own right, then the idea is pushed back, and the continuity becomes more important than the idea. Then, because there is no inherent truth or substance in the organization and it does not fulfill expectations, further effort is made in the wrong direction by pouring in more resources into building it up. Committees and procedures are proliferated, providing a pecking order for the priesthood that runs it and so eliminating the servants of the Spirit who first caught the vision.

The ultimate of this process is that, like dinosaurs and other top-heavy material structures, the organization collapses. By this time, however, the idea has too often been buried or forgotten and so, when the organization is no longer there, it appears that there is nothing left at all. Dinosaurs became extinct, because they were too big for their boots. They could not be sustained.

Dean Inge, the English churchman, wrote perceptively, "History seems to show that the powers of evil have won their greatest triumphs by capturing the organizations that were framed to defeat them, and that when the devil has thus changed the contents of the bottle he never alters the label."

Disappearance of the Medium

As the universe becomes more mentalized — that is, as its

essential nature as thought begins to shine through the mists of materiality — the medium begins to shrink. In the fields of power, communications, and knowledge, as we saw in the chapter, "The Breakup of Materialism," effectiveness has increased as they have become more ethereal, more mentalized, so that the medium has diminished. We can see, for example, that modern communications require less and less medium to contract the world into a global village. The same process is inevitable with human organizations and institutions, for their maximum effectiveness depends on the degree in which the idea, rather than its trappings, comes first. It was a wise man who remarked that the rules for every new organization should include a clause to ensure its built-in obsolescence. As this process of diminishing media continues, the horrible material process will be reversed, and the spiritual viewpoint, which sees everything as ideas, will outshine the old. In the order of Science, the build-up of a material sense of things goes wrong. Material forms are temporal. Consciousness is fundamental.

Now, the point of including some analysis of the false promises and hopes that are vested in the medium is this. Just as human beliefs and theories straddle both religious and secular interests, so too does Science. A new and scientific interpretation of the universe cannot be confined to just one side of experience. It must be all-embracing, because the lens that is used to view life embraces all that is viewed through it. We can return to the statement, "For God to know is to be." Nothing apart from this knowing and being is true. There is no outside to consciousness, for it is impossible for infinite Mind to know anything that is outside or foreign to its own nature. The world of appearance is no more than the upside down view of that which Truth is already being — a view that implies a standpoint outside Truth and so is untrue. Such a supposed view is nothing in its own right but presents, in belief, a limited view of that which is unlimited, a finite sense of that which is infinite, a distorted view of that which is held correctly in Mind.

The Fruits of the Scientific Viewpoint

When something is apprehended spiritually, that is, seen to exist in essence as idea and not as an object of physical sense, it is subject only to the Mind that is its Principle. It is not dependent on any material medium. For example, to see that intelligence, strength, supply, activity, completeness exist fundamentally as ideas in Mind, and subordinate only to Mind, is by no means an impractical approach. This is because what appears as the material medium through which these ideas are expressed, namely, education, physique, money, job, or person, is not additional to or outside consciousness. At a human level, of course, there is the medium. It is the medium divorced from the idea behind it that fails. To hold the medium as the condition or reason of something is wrong. To see it as incidental to the idea treats it in the subsidiary manner that is correct, and it will be useful so long as it is useful, and no longer. It is the dark glass, the obscuration, that gives the impression that something that exists spiritually has to be repeated materially. But this impression is not true, and it is in its disappearance through spiritual understanding, and not in building it up, that the underlying idea is experienced with greater clarity.

To understand that all that is humanly good or desirable is already embraced in "the compound idea of God, including all right ideas" is to be sure that it appears in the highest and most naturally practical way that can be appreciated at any moment. But this appearance is the illustration, not the medium. It is not substance in itself but is incidental to the fading out of the belief that substance is material and so dependent upon some organization. It is the lifting, in a degree, of "the vail that is spread over all nations." Is this not what Jesus meant when he said, "Seek ye first the kingdom of God, and his righteousness; and all these things shall be added unto you."[2] The things themselves do not belong to the kingdom, but the thoughts or ideas that they symbolize do; and the symbol remains only until it is proved redundant.

Practical Religion

Holding the illustration as incidental to the idea means that its appearance is always subservient to the Mind that has the idea. It is only by believing that the illustration is the medium, and so the substance, that the associated belief could be entertained, namely, that experience is subject to the caprice of the human mind. Ultimate reality exists without any material medium. This is practical religion for it is, as the Introduction to this book emphasised, the "binding back" of thought to some constant. This embraces every aspect of experience. To bind thought back to its divine Principle is to enjoy the reality of being, here and now, in its highest appreciable form. To bind thought to an external universe, in which the medium is more important than the idea, is to make experience subject to the unrequited toil that accompanies this mistake.

One current, and baneful, manifestation of the misuse of a medium is the present "litigious" society. Legal action to get others to behave or refrain from behaving in certain ways, or to reimburse you for hurt, is futile. The belief that there are other minds and lives in the first place is something that holds its believer in bondage to people and circumstances. When the attitude of "I'll deal with this by going to court" yields to dealing with apparent problems in and as consciousness, the result is that the ensuing action or no action will be intelligent and useful.

Mrs. Eddy writes that "Divine Science demonstrates Mind as dispelling a false sense and giving the true sense of itself, God, and the universe."[3] The Science of being is its Truth, and so that which is. It is like the coming of the dawn on earth, so irresistible and inevitable; the mists that hide the landscape are dispelled by the morning sun. In the same way, the mists, distortions, and limitations that mark the futility of mortal existence are found to be but shadows of ignorance which, with the appearing of the light of understanding, cease to hide what is already and immediately present.

13

Relationships

In every period there exists a meaning
of life, defining the highest good at which
the period aims, and in our time this
consists of the acknowledgement that the
aim of life is the union of mankind.
                                    Tolstoi

What you don't do or do to others is what
you don't do or do to yourself, because there
is one Mind.
                        Richard Dolling Wells

In the last three chapters, we have examined the role of
the medium in both a religious and secular context. The
same concept of mediumship extends beyond these larger
doctrines and issues to the detail of daily experience, and
nowhere more than in what comes under the broad heading of interpersonal relations. In fact, as we find out more
about the scientific relationship of man to God in Science,
this term is found to be self-contradictory outside of the
dream. All the "inter" words, such as intervention, intercession, interference, interdependent, and interpersonal
suggest by definition that there is something that can be
interposed between cause and its self-expression as effect.

The Unction of Love

In this context we can see the beauty of Mrs. Eddy's definition of Love, in part, as "the underived."[1] If there is a
single word that describes what is needed to offset the
friction of personal selfhood, it is the lubricant or unction
of Love. If there is one thing that can lift the veil of

human sorrow, resentment, fear, defensiveness, incompleteness, or inadequacy, it is Love, the underived. This is the understanding that the entirety of being is derived only from within itself. It exists because of itself. It is expressed as itself. Nothing is owed to, dependent on, or threatened by anything outside of itself, for no such outside exists. I, the scientific I, or Ego, do not fear, threaten, grieve for, or belittle Myself. These phases of thought are unknown to Me.

Far from entering the dream of interpersonal relations in order to shuffle the pack and produce new patterns; far from accepting the need to accept the premise of many minds, and then trying to reconcile the differing viewpoints they may hold, the one need is to bathe the situations that appear before us in that Love that loosens thought from the whole dream and lifts it out of itself to a new vision.

Love begins with the wholeness of being and not with fragments to be pieced together. Infinitely above what is called romantic love, it remains the consciousness that knows nothing but its own loveliness, harmony, and perfection. More than mere sympathy, which may join another in the slough of despond, it is expressed as the compassion, or warm-heartedness, that lifts those who turn to it above the limitations and convictions of a false viewpoint where they can see as they are seen, know as they are known, and respect themselves as they are respected. The natives of Central Africa remembered the visits of Dr. Livingstone, long after he had left them and though they had no common language, for the love he expressed which lifted them above themselves.

The Underived Knows No "Other"

Every mortal is trying to reach beyond himself or herself,

but the general belief is that this can be done only through the help of another. This, in turn, breeds a class of devoted professionals, whose lives are dedicated to helping those "others." Both, however, are accepting the premise that good in some form is to be derived from another. Both are accepting the divisibility of good into portions, with one portion at the expense of another. The oneness of being is not the premise, so it cannot find its way into the conclusion.

In Science, we have found a universe of consciousness or thought. Thoughts are related to the Mind that has the thought, and we have already seen that the consciousness of a thought remains in the Mind that thinks it. One Mind means one thinker, and so one source of thought. Thoughts do not relate to each other independently of the Mind that conceives them; nor is the substance of thought transferred from Mind to its emanation. In an earlier chapter, "How Do We Identify Man," we saw how the real man, or manifestation of Mind, is consciousness, and that when we speak of the oneness of God and man, we are referring to the correlation and coexistence of Mind and its consciousness. It is only in finding a common relationship of thought to Mind that we can then find, incidentally, the relationship of thoughts to each other. But the premise of many minds would doom this relationship from the start.

This relationship is what is meant by the "order of Science," in which Principle is above what it reflects. It is an aspect of the new paradigm, in which the very terms of reference have changed. There are three areas in the field of personal relations where this new order is becoming evident and, at the same time, bringing into view an old order that is no longer tenable and ready to be discarded.

A New Authority

One of the most obvious of these areas of change is the challenge to the established sense of authority. This is apparent in schools, in the teacher-pupil relationship; in the parent-child relationship at home; in the trade unions; in government, where the apparent deficiency of leadership that can be trusted and respected is bringing about a questioning of its right and ability to lead; and in religion, where the right and authority of priesthood in any form is becoming unacceptable.

These are wholly reassuring signs, and the impetus arises, as a previous chapter suggests, from the order of Science, in which the Principle is above its idea and is asserting itself. The old human, hierarchical order could last only so long as one believed that man, or image, had a capacity of his own, separate from his original. Within these terms of reference, the chain of command was organized much on the lines of a Roman legion, or even a football team, where one person controlled and communicated with ten, ten with a hundred, and so on. Within this structure, knowledge was power. It could be withheld, rationed, or manipulated. Thus, with power came the liability to corruption.

The "great verities of Spirit" vest power in omnipotence, communications in omnipresence, and knowledge in omniscience. There is no human appropriation of any of these verities. Already, in daily life, we can see profound changes that confirm this. Computer technology has rendered it almost impossible to hide knowledge or place it in the hands of the few. A systems approach disseminates knowledge, and so power, on a lateral instead of hierarchical basis. The buildup of personal authority has begun to give place to the child's awful realization that, in truth, "the emperor has no clothes." The poverty of human leadership is not to be lamented, because it is its very inadequacy that points to the spiritual fact that man is never a governor in the first place, and that "man governed by his creator is self-governed."[2] One Mind means one Governor.

Without this total change of framework, the pattern of history is repeated, and the basic misconception of the place where authority resides continues. There may be a change of sides, whereby the underdog has a spell as top dog, but the situation does not change fundamentally. Nor can it. True revolution does not shuffle the ingredients of an existing order. It replaces the order itself.

Two-getherness: a False Premise

Two problems that are in the forefront of contemporary thinking are divorce and war. To classify these as twin problems is not as unlikely as it might seem. Personalized, or objectified, love is the other side of the coin to personal or objective hate. To objectify, or materialize, something that exists as idea in the divine Mind is to see it through the lens of the dualistic human mind.

In this view, marriage is thought to be the coming together of two to make one. The trouble is that two-getherness can equally appear as a-part-ness. The moment you identify yourself as either a male or female, rather than as the fullness of infinite Love in self-expression, thus including all the masculine and feminine qualities that make up completeness, you effectively start divorce proceedings. You mentally put asunder that which God hath joined together. The premise being duality, the conclusion will be the same. Plurality breeds plurality, and this is just as true of an organization called the United Nations as it is of a marriage. The order of Science must be maintained. Only as we begin with the spiritual fact of the present wholeness and oneness of being will the incidental illustration be the highest institution, whether it is called marriage or any other alliance. The fundamental error in the present fabric of marriage is not that two people do not get on, but that the starting point is two people. In this sense, mortal existence is a state of divorce.

Psychology tends to accept this false premise. Counselors' offices tend to be a repository for complaints about "his or her point of view;" the assertion that he or she "thought the other was wrong;" or " I am being deprived of my rights;" "I can't live with this;" "If only he or she would change, things could be different." Such workers are then cast in the role of Solomon, trying to help, adjudicate, bring sense into a situation, or find some mental cause for anti-social behaviour. And woe betide those who put their hand in this hornet's nest, for it would keep endeavor at the level of the problem, and the dream will repeat itself in one form or another.

It would seem that, as in healing any situation, the work of the counselor will be effective to the degree that he is dealing, himself, with his own sense of things. It is letting our own consciousness be so aware of the truth, the indivisible allness of infinite Love, that what comes into our office is recognised, not as a person with a problem but as an impersonal phase of the human mind masquerading as person. It is this consciousness, rather than technique or personality, that counts and determines whether what is said is inspiring and healing. Then, instead of getting into the complexities of the hornet's nest, we let it — the upside down view — fade out in the presence of Truth. Then we are not working *with* a client, but maintaining our own conscious relationship to the divine, the only true relationship. That which comes into the presence of the Christ has to be healed. Otherwise it stays away. In this presence, there is no wrong-doer and no wronged; no accuser, no accusation, and no accused; so nothing to bear witness to a lie. In a word, we learn to see "I" to "I."

War and Divorce: the Same Mistake

The other side of "coming together" is remaining apart. Mortal existence is always at war, just as it is always in a divorce court. The basic warfare lies in the duality of the carnal, human mind which is "enmity against God." It is the whole picture of human personalization, which appears to be the place where opposites mingle and conflict. This warfare objectifies itself as the duality that divides mankind into friend and foe. This objectification is incidental to the way in which you identify yourself, for any mortal will always be fighting something, either in the name of good or against it. The fight is what matters. The spiritual answer does not lie in victory for one side or the other of duality, but in no battle.

The infinite One is not at war with itself. Only that which starts from from a basis of separation from this One finds itself at war to gain or defend a limited, portional sense of existence. To try to cure the phenomenon of war without laying the axe at its root is of little avail. It has never worked, even with the best intentions. But the spiritual fact always precedes the human perception of it. It is only from the basis of that which *is* eternally one, and not from that which has to become one, that warfare can cease. And the place where this begins is not with another but within one's own consciousness. It is here, and not over there, that the essential oneness of being is seen and experienced.

This is why we need never doubt the possibilities of thought in harmony with its Principle, nor question whether the problems of the world are too big and complex for any individual to influence. There are not big and small problems; multiple or single issues. There is one problem, which is the wrong lens, and this itself is mythological. There can, in fact, be no standpoint outside the focal distance of infinity, and no interpretation can take place other than that of Principle. The order of Science brings with it innate harmony. The loss of the keynote of being results from a mistake and appears as discord. But the substance of the discord does not lie with the phenomenon but in the mistake, and this itself is nothing.

The new paradigm refers to a state of thought that proceeds and interprets everything from a totally new standpoint, namely, that of the divine Mind, or Principle, itself. It demands the most revolutionary thinking that has ever been, for everything that is based on a departure from this order is rendered null and void. It denotes a revolution of thought, not just of circumstances, and it leaves nothing standing where it was before.

14

Mind-Healing

This is the great error of the day, that
physicians separate the soul from the body.
Plato

Be noble, and the nobleness that lies
in other men, sleeping, but never dead,
will rise in majesty to meet thine own.
Lowell

Spiritual and Faith Healing

The difference between metaphysical healing and what comes under the general banner of spiritual or faith healing is great. The ability to heal metaphysically comes from an understanding of its Science, a consecrated life, an unselfed love, and the apprehension of the divine nature. No mortal would lay claim to have progressed far along this path. The fact that healings have taken place which have been unequalled since the first century shows that "a grain of Christian Science does wonders for mortals." The final chapter in Science and Health contains testimonies of people who have been healed of almost every kind of disease just by reading the book. And the publication, a hundred years later, of "A Century of Christian Science Healing" shows that Truth has lost none of its healing power.

Metaphysical healing is infinitely more than alternate medicine. It does not include laying on hands or any physical manipulation; its method does not focus on the person in need but on the presence of God; its prayers are not supplications to a far-off God; nor are they even a matter of one person praying for another, but an acknowledgement of the immanent nature of Mind-power. While it is encouraging to note the many churches today which are recognizing that the Master Christian's first demand on his followers was to heal the sick, it has to be said that the methods employed differ greatly from the metaphysical.

The Physical Is Really Mental

Fundamental to the practice of true spiritual healing is an understanding of the mental nature of what appears as a material condition. Like any other problem, sickness and sin are not solved within the terms of reference where they occur. To accept the picture of a sick or sinning mortal body, and then to try to change that material picture through some mental activity called prayer, makes strong demands upon credibility. If any results do occur this way, they will not be on a scientific or permanent basis but will saviour more of blind faith or mesmerism. The former would reflect the efforts, entirely sincere, of those who invoke the intervention of a personal God on behalf of someone dear, or even some world situation, that is suffering. The latter, again however sincere the motive, could result only in changing the dream picture from a belief of sickness to one of health without establishing health on an unchallenged basis of understanding. A practitioner of hypnotism might well achieve just such an effect but would readily admit that the mental framework of thought, within which the likelihood that this or some other disability could occur, is unchanged. The duality of the human mind would ensure this.

There is now a more general admission that thinking affects the material body, and hence the recognition of a growing list of diseases that are classified as psychosomatic. While the peculiarly Western habit of treating a physical body as something apart from the patient's mind is being found inadequate, the quantum leap is not taken whereby both this mind and its embodiment, or body, are understood to be one problem and one myth. The so-called mortal ego, together with the ills that it conceives and contains, is a package deal. They cannot be dealt with separately. It is not possible to accept identity as this ego and then try to put right what is wrong with it. The scientific approach, in which the divine Principle must do the interpreting, is the only way in which the "package deal" is seen to be no part of the divine Mind, or Life, and so is itself mesmerism. "The material body, which you call *me*, is mortal mind."[1]

Mind-healing has to be more than prayer to a personal God; more than the mental manipulation of a patient's mind; more than positive thinking; and certainly more than self-delusion. Indeed, if it depended in any way on the human mind, instead of enjoying the correct view of the divine Mind, how would one explain the healing of animals or "non-personal events." For example, in the writer's own experience, he has seen the protection of many hundreds of young plants in a greenhouse, when not a single one was lost after they had inadvertently been sprayed with a potent weed-killer. On another occasion, after the blossoms on a large fruit farm had been killed by an untimely frost, all the blossoms on that and a neighbouring farm grew again. A cyclone, heading towards a city where friends lived, suddenly turned off at a right angle, only a few miles from the shore, and spent itself over the ocean. And — as reported in the local newspapers — the home of a Christian Science teacher was protected when a forest fire, fanned by a strong wind, suddenly stopped at his border fence line. If health, or wholeness, is an idea of God, then it is a law to be demonstrated as scientifically and unerringly as any other law. If it is not demonstrated, then the fault is not with the law but with the practitioner's incomplete understanding of it.

The Separation of the Moral and Physical

A medical practitioner accepts that his prime field of work is a physical one. While he may accept that there are other factors, such as the psychological, to be considered, he would not feel it was his province to touch on the moral state of the patient. He works within clear terms of reference, and does so in a way that is dedicated and often self-sacrificing. No one should decry or criticize this work, and any reluctance to use his services would be based upon the realization that one's problem lies in consciousness, not in the body. But the desire to relieve suffering could certainly not be questioned.

A churchman sees his prime field of work to be the soul rather than the body of man. The moral side is indeed included within his terms of reference, but to an extent that the sins, rather than the ills, of mankind have occupied his efforts; and the physical demands upon the Christian have tended to be relegated to the physician. The moral and the physical, which Jesus saw to be one, are separated. This has meant that, in the main, such statements by Christ Jesus as, "Wherefore by their fruits ye shall know them;"[2] "Go ye into all the world;" and "Heal the sick..."[3] have been ignored, and the responsibility for carrying out these demands has been handed over to those who have often never heard them.

The attention now being paid to the conduct of healing services and the laying on of hands is still in the realm of applying spiritual truth to physical problems. Notwithstanding this general trend, it should be acknowledged that there have always been notable examples of true spiritual healing as a consequence of holy, uplifted thought, and one can think of the great divines of the Mediaeval Church, the case histories of healing by prayer recorded at Iona Abbey and, of course, the early Christians, whose ability to heal was a prerequisite to their joining the church.

The Christ Healing

In Science, sickness is the disguise; the error is sin. Sin, in its final definition, is the belief that mind and life are separate from God. Sickness is inherent in this belief. This is why Science heals both sin and sickness by the same method. It is not trying just to improve the conditions of the dream of material existence but to despoil the dream of identity. An important statement, which reflects the way in which Jesus did his great and unparallelled works, is found in Science and Health, "We must realize the ability of mental might to offset human misconceptions and to replace them with the life which is spiritual, not material."[4] Healing from this basis starts from the premise that the only Life is here and now; that it is always wholly spiritual and is just as the one Mind knows it. This Life is the only Life of man and is as unchangeable and perfect as the Mind that conceives and constitutes it. Consequently, the material picture of sin, sickness, lack, and death is to be seen, not as actual, material conditions but as mental misconceptions of the one and only Life. These misconceptions would have the same substance and reality as the apparently bent stick reflected in the water, or the distorted image in a fun-mirror. Their suppositional presence could not occupy space, any more than would a misconception of some mathematical fact or a ghost. They would stay in the realm of illusion.

Treating "Patients"

The example of Jesus' ministry, and of those who followed him in the immediate centuries afterwards, shows the effectiveness of treating material pictures in this way. For example, the treatment of lack, which besets so many today, appeared then as the feeding of five thousand hungry people. Were there really all those mouths to feed, or did the five loaves and two fishes, so ample for one, typify the plenitude of the one, indivisible, and spiritual Life that had never been conditioned by matter? Was this so-called miracle just the producing of material substance? There are many, particularly in the East, who understand the mental nature of what we call matter who are able to perform such displays.

Jesus' work was the scientific proof that the mental misconception called lack was located only in an inadequate human standpoint of perception. This misconception had nothing to do with the divine Mind, in the presence of which both the wrong standpoint, and the misconception it included, had to disappear. In this disappearance, the inadequacy of the material view of existence yielded to the understanding of the abundant nature of the divine Life, always present. That which was true for one had to be true for all because of the indivisible nature of the infinite. An idea like abundance could no more be appropriated personally or divided than an idea like "six" or "seven." Ideas cannot be rationed. Indeed the events of that momentous day did not involve the setting aside of physical laws by means of prayer, but the offsetting of mental misconceptions through the divine Mind's true concept of being. The physical appearance was simply the fading out of a limited sense of things that was hiding from itself the abundance that was never absent to the correct view.

Good Not Miraculous

The law of good and wholeness was evident in so many

ways in the career of Jesus; but the so-called miracles have to be seen as incidental to the Christ-consciousness, and so to the laws of eternal Truth, rather than signs of some personal dispensation, if they are to be relevant to this period and practiced on a scientific basis. That which heals is always the correct view of the divine Mind and not a person tinkering with a wrong view. Hence the command to "let this mind be in you which was also in Christ Jesus."[5] Hence, too, the moral and spiritual demands made on those who would attempt to heal by his methods.

The storm that threatened to engulf Jesus and his disciples on the Lake of Galilee; the deaf, dumb, blind, and crippled whom he healed; the sinners whom he forgave; and the dead whom he raised were, to the Mind that was God (and that was all there was to his consciousness), nothing other than mental misconceptions and so non-existent in reality. They were to be offset by the might of omnipotence – of God – as unchallenged power. In every case, the healing was not an event that took place at the level where it seemed to occur. It was always a mental result of the fading out of a false, limited, upside-down view of things in the presence of Truth. God-with-us as consciousness offset the misconception of God not with us. Such healing was never mind over matter, but the divine Mind present in place of the human mind and the misconceptions *it* contained.

It should be clear that no sensible individual is going to insult the sick with the statement that there is nothing wrong with them, and that their problems are all illusion. If he can heal them, there is no need to tell them. But, if explanation is helpful, then he can agree that sickness and suffering are horribly real to that which is sick and suffers. Then it can be pointed out that, while at that level it all seems so real, there is a higher level — the level at which the divine Mind, and not the human, is knowing —

where none of this suffering is going on. It is like talking with a man who lives in a two-dimensional world. It would be pointless telling him that his horizons are false and his limitations illusory. But it would be possible to say, "Supposing you accepted different parameters, involving three, instead of two, dimensions. You might just find that what appeared so real and constricting at the first level is seen not to apply at the second." The clarity of the divine Mind touches and lifts the patient out of his bondage.

As we have seen, it is because thought is basic that the sense of something *is* that thing. The material condition, therefore, is never solid substance but solid conviction. If it were material substance, how could one explain the healing of a growth or a broken bone? I recall the occasion when the ten-year old sister of one of my soldiers was knocked down by a motor cycle. When he heard the news, she had already been unconscious in hospital for twelve hours. She had a concussion, a fractured skull, a fractured jaw-bone, and severe lacerations. Christian Science prayer was given and, in the morning, not only was she conscious, but there was also no trace of a fracture in the skull. The jaw was healed in a day or so, before the doctors touched it. Although her teeth had cut deeply into her lips, no scar was left. The prognosis was a long stay in hospital, and the local council law insisted that she remain under observation for three weeks. It was understood that the only law operating was the law of God, and she was released after ten days – in time to sit for some examinations she would otherwise have missed.

Healing the "Cat"

There is no incurable disease. Incurability is unchanged thought, either that of the patient or the general mental atmosphere. A bone is no more substantial than a milk pudding or a theorem, and that is why it can be healed by spiritual means. The harder cases require only a greater understanding that nothing exists materially but just as misconceived thought. The problem is never the physical disguise it is wearing but is always the human mind, just as the experiences of a dream have no validity outside of the dream mind. They are not true to real consciousness. A Christian Science teacher once remarked, "When a cat meets a dog, and the cat arches its back, you remove the dog. You don't treat the cat for curvature of the spine." In spiritual healing, the "dog" is the human, mortal mind, and it is the removal of this, and not an attempt to change "the cat," that is involved.

Leavening the Lump

Mind healing takes place primarily in the healer's thought, or rather, the Mind that is divine dissolves the belief that there is a second mind, called practitioner or patient, to hide what is. As the thought of the healer stays in constant relation to the divine, the spiritual, and the eternal, this thought ceases to be human and takes on the scope and efficacy of the divine Mind. As the pictures of sin, sickness, and mortality are banished from the con-sciousness of the healer, this will appear as healing and enlightenment wherever there is expectant and receptive thought, including — but not exclusive to — that of the patient.

The use of the phrase " receptive thought" raises the ques-tion of why prayer does not always seem to heal. Merely to reply that medical and other healing methods also have their failures begs the question. The Principle does not fail, even though the practitioner may appear to do so. In Science, it is important to remember that the message is not just that there is a spiritual existence that is true and that, as we learn more of this truth, our human lives will improve. It is that there is only one Life, which is spiritual now, and in the understanding of this Life both the belief in another existence and the consciousness that believes it fade out. This constitutes what is called healing.

To measure Truth in terms of what it appears incidentally to do in human affairs would be the same as measuring the effectiveness of the sun in terms of what it is doing to darkness. At one level it may appear that some shadows dissolve more readily than others. At another, we see that the sun is simply engaged in shining, and shadows are no part of its presence or experience. At a human level, it would certainly seem that certain states of thought militate against healing more than others. Bigotry, stolidity, self-righteousness, human will, all oppose Truth.

An unexpected illustration of non-receptive thought, not without its irony, occurred when I was asked to take over the care of a man who was suffering from arthritis, as the practitioner who had been helping was going away. The patient was not an easy character, and at the end of the week he was no better. However, his eyesight had so improved that he could read the smallest print from the telephone book without his spectacles. When his practitioner returned, he complained, "But, I never asked him to heal my eyesight!" The fact was that Truth got in where it could. Having said that, one finds it is still important to remember that Mind-healing, as suggested above, is not primarily concerned with how or when light lightens the darkness, but with the fact that, in infinite light, there is no darkness at all. It is from this standpoint that true metaphysical work takes place.

Jesus certainly found that, in some places, he could do no great works because of peoples' unbelief. The determination to accept Truth's message only for what it might hopefully do to meet human needs — in other words, to place oneself mentally at the receiving end of good — does not help. But, in the final analysis, the practitioner of this Science can only say, in complete humility, "The little I can prove still points to an unchanging and infinitely available law of good, and as I let the divine understanding, which is all that is true, BE my thinking, so all will appear to me as the one Mind is seeing it. And in this seeing there is no problem to put right."

Jesus said, "I, if I be lifted up from the earth, will draw all men unto me."[6] More than just a referral to the cross, this statement surely confirmed that if I lift up what I accept as I, or consciousness, from the level of material thinking, I will draw all that is within the orbit of my experience into the same state of Mind that I AM. Ideas are universal and, to work in the realm of ideas, is to include the specific need in a more universal understanding. Thus is the entire lump of human thought leavened, and this explains the phenomenon of the same progressive idea appearing in many places at the same time without any visible organization behind it. It also explains why it is as easy to heal those who are at a distance from the healer as those who are present. To the one, universal Mind, there is no "here" or "there." All that is true of what A and B think of themselves or each other is what I, Mind, know of Myself. This universal knowing appears, incidentally, as the receptive, expectant thought being touched, not only in the case of the patient, but universally. Good is not personal.

While, in healing, the objects of sense are exchanged for spiritual ideas, this is far more than mental gymnastics. There is no intellectual formula and no domination of one mind by another. Spiritual healing demands that we abide in that altitude of consciousness that is aware only of the eternal laws of the divine Principle. This Principle is not just something to which we turn in time of crisis but is the yardstick against which we detect and mentally dismiss anything that does not reflect it in daily life. Then healing is a matter of grace, not labour. As Mrs. Eddy once said, "You will give off God naturally as a flower gives off perfume. I have healed hundreds in this way."

The humanly Christian character is, of its own, not sufficient to heal, but this character, combined with the understanding of the divine nature, unobscured by any belief that there is a second, human power to work good or ill, is essential. The Love and Truth that heal, and that are the power behind Mind-healing, mean more than the unselfish love that requires another to whom one can be unselfish. It is the unselfed love that contains no human sense of self to stand in the way, thus removing all that would try to hide what already exists. The Love that recognises nothing outside its own loveliness, that is too pure to behold evil, and that is light, containing no darkness at all, knows nothing outside its own, infinite presence to heal. And that is why it heals.

15

Healing the World

If a Clod bee washed away by the Sea,
Europe is the lesse, as well as if a
Promentorie were, as well as if a Manor
of thy Friends, or if thine own were.
No man is an Island intire of itselfe.
John Donne

Involvement in the problems and needs of society and of the world is today more widespread than ever before. Even though it might appear sometimes that self-interest and selfishness are likewise spreading, this is certainly an age of concern. In Britain, for example, each of the three major charitable organizations has more members than any political party. Social issues begin to take precedence over politics. Disillusion with government from outside is matched by a new sense of individual responsibility. Compassion extends beyond the immediate neighbourhood and embraces the needy in other lands. Involvement in trying to solve environmental problems is reaching the political arena itself. There is hardly an aspect of human, animal, or natural life that does not command its supporters.

Love of Neighbours

From the standpoint of Science, all this is natural and inevitable. We can recall the statement, "All that is true is a sort of necessity, a portion of the primal reality of things."[1] That which is eternally true is the oneness of being — its integrity and indivisibility. To love your neighbour as yourself, rather than just as your neighbour, is more than morally desirable; it is a spiritual necessity, since what you see of your neighbour *is* yourself. As the New England saying goes, "The man I see is the man I be." From the standpoint of the only I, or Ego, the stream must be as pure as the fount. In other words, the same source does not produce love and hate, respect and criticism, safety and fear, or any of the opposites of the human view. To admit a sense of anything "out there" is to accept it as "here," since the consciousness of something is all there is to it. To admit the actuality or possibility of some error in another is to accept its likelihood in one's own experience and to accept it as "I." On the other hand, to refuse it entry into the consciousness that I AM, is the way for it to disappear as our neighbour. Religion and Science combine in stating that Love is the fulfilling of the law, since nothing less can express the unity of being.

The same is true when it comes to environmental concerns. The involvement in ecological problems can appear only because the spiritual fact behind the apparent conflict of interests in the environment is the same oneness of being. The appearance of the ecumenical movement reflects the instinctive feeling that "Our Father which art in heaven" should appear as love, rather than dissension, on earth. The assertion of equal social rights for women and others who have been disadvantaged in the past expresses the existing fact of the self-completeness of man as the self-expression of creative Mind. One Mind does not place a portion of itself at a disadvantage, nor does it abuse, suppress, or conflict with itself. And, in politics and industry, the trend towards internationalism and transnational agreements arises from the fact that the truth behind it already exists. That which is necessary appears at every level of experience.

What Blights Human Effort?

The question arises, Why do so many of these right endeavours go wrong? At one level, this would certainly appear to be the case. Endeavour to produce unity, such as in the United Nations operations, meets reversal. The breakdown of the Berlin Wall and the removal of the Iron Curtain did not result in freedom from problems. Women's rights movements have resulted in the amendment of some discriminating laws but also in an imbalance between the behavioural pattern of men and women in other ways. And the best intentions of environmentalists seem thwarted by the age-old forces of selfishness and greed. The bigness of the idea tends to get dwarfed in the smallness of personalities.

It is at this point that we should remember the basic assertion in this book that it is not what we see but how we see it that determines experience. If you wear a pair of red spectacles, then everything you see will be coloured. To see a million red people would be no more a cause for alarm than to see one, since the redness would not be in the object but in the lens that is being used. When that lens is the distorting human mind, then all that is seen through it will reflect the distortion and ambivalence of that viewpoint. It cannot present other than an upside down view of reality. Thus, so long as it is retained as the acceptable way of perceiving an individual, a nation, a world, or the environment, the picture will never be correct, despite the efforts to change it. You cannot correct the image in a distorting mirror except by changing the mirror.

It is for this reason that good people have tried without much success to change the universe in which they live. Some problems are solved; new ones appear. For example, as the Introduction mentioned, the social reforms of

Lord Shaftesbury in England removed the more iniqui-
tous forms of bondage in the employment of children. But
a *sense* of bondage is as palpable as ever and will remain
so, as long as we believe that there is an external universe,
outside consciousness, to which we will always be in
bondage in one way or another. The efforts to save the
rain forests, at present thwarted by vested interests, will
continue to be abortive so long as it is phenomena, rather
than human nature, that are the focus of attention. The
attempt to produce unity out of many, whether in politics
or elsewhere, cannot succeed so long as the starting point
is plurality instead of the oneness that already is. In every
case, the desirable evidence of reform can appear only
when it is incidental to the fading out of a wrong viewpoint, or lens, before the everlasting spiritual facts. This is
the scientific way which, instead of merely producing a
change of appearance, lets appearance yield to understanding. It is never a better human condition, but a less
human, limited, distorted view of the one and only condition that already exists, that is our concern.

Try It!

To those who may feel this is unsubstantiated optimism,
the reply would be, Try it! For too long, as surely any
thinking individual would agree, we have tried to do
everything except change the lens through which we perceive. It has not worked, and the crises in the world must
open thought to a new approach. But then someone may
ask, What can I, as one individual do? There are three
answers to this. The first is, that you do not indulge in a
mathematical mistake, just because everyone else accepts
it. The buck always stops here. Change in others by individual example is well-known. The second is, that the
truth always precedes the human mind's perversion of it.
This is why the truth is a necessity. We work from the
standpoint of that which *is* one, and not that which has to

be *made* one. "The earth is the Lord's, and the fullness thereof."[2]

But the third, and most important, answer is that there is not anything but "I" to think rightly. If we wait for a he, she, or they to conform, we deny what I AM. In fact we do not have to change a materially sick universe any more than an invalid, a failing business, or a failing crop. We change the lens through which we look at the one universe. The holdup has not been because we cannot do this, but because we have accepted a difference between small problems within our capacity and others that are not. Yet the principle that 2x2=4 is the same when we speak of millions. The restriction is self-imposed and needless. When Jesus made his profound statement that "the kingdom of heaven is within you," he was certainly reminding his listeners that this kingdom was always within the correct perception of being and that, in consequence, there was nothing in it that needed changing. Then, just as in healing a sick person, the consciousness of the present wholeness of being causes the belief in its opposite to yield. For example, there can be no gap in the ozone layer in the understanding of omnipresence. The ideas of unity, completeness, beauty, renewal, preservation, and safety that constitute this consciousness and operate universally and indivisibly, assert themselves and leaven the lump of human ignorance. Then, as with individuals, the incidental appearing has to be social, civil, political, and religious codes that enhance, instead of divide, man's existence.

Misconceptions Exposed

By beginning with God, the divine Mind or Principle, which is the only scientific approach, the apparent duality of compassionate concern, on the one hand, and callous selfishness, on the other, is reconciled. As a sense of the oneness of universal being dawns upon human thought, it appears that its opposite is highlighted at the same time. In the same way, switching on a light in a disused room brings to view the cobwebs and dust that have to be swept away. The apparent opposite of the highest right is still the highest right seen from an upside down standpoint. This is why wrong does not challenge, nor is it an alternative to, right. It is right misconceived, since right is all there is. Thus the apparent greed, competition, and selfishness of identity as a human self are simply the inversion of the only self or identity which is wholly spiritual. False identity comes to the surface only that its futility, ugliness, and falsity can be self-seen and self-destroyed. But the spiritual fact, of which this false identity is the inversion, remains untouched.

Our One Responsibility

There is no race towards the alternatives of a millennium or Armageddon. Moreover, salvation is individual experience; the experience of the kingdom does not depend on others or external circumstances. Ultimately, the one thing for which we are responsible is the concept of the universe and our fellow man that we retain. Far from ignoring the needs of either, this spiritual awareness of what is true, inevitably though incidentally, appears as the wisdom, perception, and compassion to do the humanly kind and necessary thing — but without being mentally touched by it. In the Gospel stories, we read frequently that Jesus felt "compassion," but never sympathy. The latter involves getting mentally into the ditch where we see another lying. Compassion is the warmth of heart that lifts the sufferer out of the ditch into a higher appreciation of his innate worth and wholeness. To love the world and one's neighbour as oneself is to let the consciousness of Love embrace all we see; to see man whole and upright, instead of fallen and disgraced; and to see the new heaven and new earth as present experience. The Christ takes human thought where it finds it and lifts it higher.

Today, mass communications convey mass problems by mass media to mass audiences. But there is no mass answer. Only an individual one. Whether the picture is one of disease or famine, corruption of children through drugs, or the plight of the increasing numbers of the elderly, the threat of war or environmental disasters, the correct view, which alone heals, is always here and not over there. We do not give our permission to be mesmerized.

So where do we start? The answer is with number one. The fact is that Christ Jesus, more than anyone in recorded history, walked on the water, quelled storms, overcame distance and time, and fed the multitude. He is the example. Only if his record was the exception would we be justified in ignoring it. But, if it is the example, then we should no more prevent ourselves from taking the first, simple steps of proof than a pupil in an arithmetic class would renounce the science of mathematics because he cannot at once study calculus. We may start small, but we must think big. Everyone has to start somewhere. We start with "I." We start by recognising the presence of one Mind in our family or in our work. We start by recognising the one Life whenever and wherever we go, whether it is in our home, our garden, when we go for a walk, or when we have to deal with the pictures of blight, disease, or death. We start by watching thought here, instead of waiting for the other fellow over there to make the first move. In short, Try it! And don't be surprised if it works!

Acts of God

The world of our consciousness includes more than even the most optimistic human would think was within his power. There is a whole class of problems, often referred to as "acts of God" which beset humanity, even if then that same God is beseeched for aid in offsetting the effects of that for which He is held responsible. Earthquakes, floods, famine, hurricanes, and the eruption of volcanoes, are not generally assumed to be disasters that can be averted. At best, the experts try to forecast their likelihood. Yet all these phenomena form part of the mental atmosphere that makes up our universe, and the failure to deal with them as one would other problems does not lie in the fact that it cannot be done, but in the lack of attention that has been paid to the possibility. Yet, if the mesmerism of the human mind can produce an apparent storm in the Indian port, surely the divine Mind is the greater power that can offset this mesmerism. Some examples have been given in Chapter 14.

In fact, there is much evidence in Bible history of prophets, or men who perceived what was going on with spiritual, not material, sense, offsetting storms and other "natural" disasters. Elijah summed up the reason for this in the words that "the Lord [which always stood for the spiritual sense of things] was not in the wind ...the earthquake... or the fire."[3] And certainly the same law of dominion is present, and is being demonstrated in some degree today, in the many recorded examples when scientific prayer has preempted or annulled the effects of these disasters.

Spiritual Safety

In Biblical history, wind has symbolized both destruction and the omnipotence of God. Earthquakes have signified the overturning of mental attitudes. Fire has stood for purification. Mrs. Eddy speaks of "the volcanoes of partizanship."[4] But, while reducing all these to mental instead of physical phenomena, the need is to understand that a mental climate does not *cause* disasters; it constitutes them, and so they are mental states, not physical occurrences with a mental cause. And, always, the mesmerism is less than the divine Mind.

Thus, we can read, with a certain equanimity, the prophecies of Christ Jesus that the time would come when the signs of the end of the world would be wars and rumours of wars, famines, pestilences, earthquakes, and "the abomination of desolation."[5] He foresaw the shaking and overturning of a false sense of the world, but only because the true, spiritual sense existed already. So he could say that "when ye see these things come to pass, look up, and lift up your heads... the kingdom of God is nigh at hand." Rather obviously, it is only the shakeable that can be shaken. That which is permanent cannot be shaken, because it is. So all that can disappear is a precarious and mistaken sense of the one Life and universe.

Science and Health forecasts a similar mental fermentation which "will continue until all errors of belief yield to understanding... The more material the belief, the more obvious its error, until divine Spirit, supreme in its domain, dominates all matter, and man is found in the likeness of Spirit, his original being."[6] Knowing that the life and substance of everything exist in their Principle and are therefore safe, we need not be concerned nor involved in the self-destruction of error. In abiding in Principle, our identity is always with that which is doing the overturning , and never with what is being overturned. Man's safety does not lie in the attempt to avert the forces of destruction at the level where they seem to occur, but in living above that level, where there has never been an alternative to safety. Jesus referred to this level as "my kingdom [which] is not of this world." Yet it was sufficiently practical to surmount the unkind forces of this world, both on his own behalf and that of others.

The greatest contribution anyone can make today is to show by example the way of escape from identification with the self-destroying forces of evil. People everywhere seek this example and assurance. This is far more than concern for the environment of a material universe. It is the recognition and proof that the only universe is spiritual, forever untouched by any misconceptions about it. We know the importance of not being taken in by "the fear of fear." In like manner, we learn not to be deluded by the mesmerism of mesmerism. To recognise the forces of evil as mesmerism is to recognise them as nothing, and thus to find our ability to deal with them from the standpoint of the omnipotence, omnipresence, and omniscience of infinite Love.

16

Life Not Death

That which is can never cease to be;
that which is not will not exist. To see
this truth of both is theirs who part essence
from accident, substance from shadow.
Indestructible, learn thou ! the Life is,
spreading life through all. It cannot
anywhere, by any means, be anywise
diminished, stayed or changed.
                    The Song Celestial

Because the popular and educated view of life is confined to the interval between birth and the grave, mankind has been preoccupied either with preparing for a life after death or speculating about what this future life might be like. Theology, seeing the present world as little more than a preparatory school for the future, takes the first option. Actions today are accounted for tomorrow. Physical science tries to prevent or delay the transition. Some schools of political thought, believing in no future existence, confine their effort to arranging fair shares in the only kingdom they admit. Curiosity about a possible future is widespread.

All these attitudes stem from the basic assumption that mortal life — a phrase that is self-contradictory because it literally means "dead" life — is the actuality of existence. Its very frailty leads thought to seek something better and more durable. "Mortals are believed to be here without their consent and to be removed as involuntarily, not knowing why nor when."[1] The span and nature of such existence are hard to reconcile with an understanding of Life.

158

The Train Journey of Existence

The process between cradle and grave can be likened to a train journey, with the passengers moving along a course that leads through this life to, it is hoped, something beyond. On the way, there are a number of stations, thresholds of experience, human milestones. At some unexpected and unpredictable point along the line, there is a big junction, with a sign "All Change." We surmise the journey will continue until a range of conditions has been met, but we cannot be certain of this. We do know, however, that once we board, it is hard not to stay there.

The starting point of this journey is mortality, but we hope to find immortality at the end. Beginning with physicality, we hope to achieve spirituality. We note that, because the passengers on the train are just fragments of existence, called mortal persons, their experience of the journey — the other passengers, the scenery, the stations, and events on the way — is all external to themselves, so that they can exercise little control over it. Indeed, far from just taking a ride on the train, they are being taken for a ride by it!

Creeping Death

It is only as we learn that the underlying substance of everything is consciousness, not matter or time, that the basic error of premise is uncovered. All that can die or dissolve is matter, and when it is understood that matter is "theoretical mind," or illusion, then the whole basis of death is undermined. When we reduce all to thought, it is apparent that ideas, rules, or laws are, as we saw in an earlier chapter, eternal. There is no death or limitation in them. On the other hand, beliefs, or thoughts which do not emanate from the divine Mind, do not have life, because they lack the essential ingredients of Truth. They are "death thoughts," and they lead in turn to their acute form called the grave. Such thoughts as fear, hate, dishonesty, criticism, envy, lust, and so on, are death in slow motion, or creeping death. Thoughts, or ideas, such as joy, abundance, peace, love, are Life thoughts and constitute immortality.

No Past or Future

Moreover, in recognising all to be consciousness, we find that everything is now. A memory is a present state of thought calling itself a past. A fear is a present state calling itself a future. The difference between life and death is certainly a state of consciousness, but it is also now. As Paul put it, "to be carnally minded is death; but to be spiritually minded is life and peace."[2] Since, then, it is how we are "minded" that determines between Life and death, it is here and now, and not there and after, that we begin to rise from the dead and prove our present immortality. Man, as the manifestation or consciousness of the divine Mind, "does not cross the barriers of time into the vast forever of Life, but he coexists with God and the universe."[3] From this standpoint of present perfection and immortality, progress is seen as the passing off or yielding of beliefs that obscure what is, and not the passing on of persons into some other sphere of existence. Only by postponing the present practice of Life do we place it in the future. Thoreau was right when he said that " God Himself culminates in the present moment, and will never be more divine in the lapse of all the years."

The Lesson of the Train

The discovery that Life is, always has been, and always will be the I AM, is simple, though so radical to human thought that the implication of its fundamental message can easily be overlooked. And this message is that we are not on the train; nor is there any train. Our mental starting point, therefore, is not an acceptance of the conditions attached to the journey, followed by an attempt to alleviate them. Instead, we find that, because of the eternal co-existence of Principle and its idea, the conditions and experiences of the journey, as well as that which appears to undergo it, have nothing to do with the I AM. They are no part of true identity. Omnipresence does not have to go anywhere to be omnipresent. The death-process starts with a material birth that no mortal remembers. It continues with the experience of toil, limitation, and fear in an environment he cannot explain. And it ends with an event over which he has no control. This has nothing to do with Life and the reality it includes. It is just a ghost story, with the mortal ego as the ghost.

It is in the understanding of present and eternal Life that the whole of mortal existence is found to be a dream. The dreamer is the carnal mind, or mesmerism. The pictures of its dream, which never leave the mind that authors them, are like the characters and events of a novel which never leave the mind of their author. They appear as persons, places, things, episodes, relationships, pains and pleasures, hopes and disappointments, and all the futility and inadequacy that constitute the train journey of material existence. So, is it better to stay in the dream to help the passengers with their trials, or to understand that there are no passengers? There is no requirement to dream the dreamer's dream, and it is only in the fading out of the composite myth called dreamer and dream that the apparent conditions that are attached to it yield to the ever-presence and fullness of the one Life. The promise of "Life more abundantly" refers to less dream — not an improved one.

Reincarnation

As progress is measured in terms of dropping off a personal sense of identity separate from God, a new look can be taken at the whole subject of reincarnation, something that occupies the theories and attention of large portions of mankind. Science has to take issue with this because it refutes the belief that anything true is incarnate in matter in the first place, and therefore that it could be reincarnated in matter in the second. It is the basic belief that life, substance, or intelligence was ever inherent in matter that has to dissolve; and this dissolution, which takes place in thought, is not conditioned or accelerated by physical death.

Karma

This leads to an analysis of what might be termed the cycle of retribution or karma. If this is determined by matter or time, then it would be reasonable to presume that you pay the last farthing either now or later for every wrong that you have done. Likewise, the reward for any good will be found on the same balance sheet of time. But, when everything is seen to be consciousness, then it is that alone which constitutes an individual's hell or heaven at any moment. Right carries its own reward with it; wrong likewise. Failure to do things right now means that the consciousness of wrong doing continues for so long as that failure persists, but no longer. The only absolution from wrong is the cessation of wrong. And that is always here: here-now, or here-after, but always here. The wrong done to another is always the wrong done to oneself, for it entails the admission of wrong into one's consciousness. In the end, all that is inevitable is good, for the only power of evil is to uncover itself, be self-seen, and so self-destroyed. It is infinite Love that does not permit the consciousness of one farthing's worth of error, and this is the truth about what appears as paying the last farthing.

Someone I knew in England worked in a store where she had to handle money. She found Science and, as she studied, the new understanding began to change her life. Physical problems disappeared; she met a man whom she soon married. They had a happy home, and a baby was on the way. Then everything seemed to crash. She was found stealing money and instantly dismissed. The basis of trust and respect in the home was shaken; their income, now that she was without work, was insufficient to maintain their home; she had a miscarriage, and the clouds appeared to have no silver lining.

She came for a talk and was reminded of the inherent sinlessness of her divine nature, which had never been impugned. While it was made clear that sin and its punishment went hand in hand, it was always a matter of an error destroying itself, and not of a person paying a penalty. Though no repetition of this error could be countenanced, the punishment could last only so long as the identification with the sin and sinner remained. The punishment ceases when there is nothing to punish, and it is the error and not person that merits it.

Shortly after this talk, she was telephoned by the manager of the store and was offered not only a new job with increased responsibility but also a large sum of money to compensate her for what they felt to have been an unfair dismissal. And this was, spiritually speaking, true, for there was nothing in the real man to be accused. Once the complete disassociation from the sin and sinner was acknowledged, there was no penalty and no one to pay it. Harmony was restored in the home; a new baby arrived; and some understanding of the true nature of Love and absolution was gained.

Was this a "soft option?" There is no easy way out for that thought which identifies with sin by indulging it, for the sin and its penalty go hand in hand. On the other hand, when the error is exterminated in consciousness, it is surely better to begin life at a new and freer level than to have a sense of human retribution attached to that which has mentally outgrown the mistake. It was to the adulterous woman, whom the onlookers wished to stone, that Christ Jesus said, "Neither do I condemn thee: go, and sin no more."[4] Does the teacher of mathematics penalize the pupil for the mistake that has been made or rejoice in its correction?

Near-Death Experience

Life never has been contingent on matter, and the dream experience has no more relationship to Life than the belief that two times two is five has to the fact it is four. In this connection it is interesting to note the publication of several books which recount the experience of people who have been pronounced clinically dead but who have been revived. In every case, the common experience was that they found themselves separate from the body that had apparently died, yet with an unchanged ability to see, hear, and move physically. The only difference lay in an inability to communicate with those who thought they had died, because they were in a different dream of existence.

The inference is threefold. First it is clear that, instead of inhabiting a material body which, in turn, dictates the conditions of existence, those who have been pronounced dead still embrace their sense of body in their thought, and so can dictate terms to it. Second, they find that what they thought had killed their body had not touched the mind that included that body. But, though they might be freed of a particular disease or accident, this would not mean freedom from a material body until the thought about that body changed. And, third, they would be no more spiritual as a result of the experience unless they had drawn the conclusion that Life never had been in matter to die or be resurrected.

Life Not Contingent on Matter

A lady in her eighties was gravely ill, and her next of kin were informed she could not last more than a short time. A Christian Science practitioner was called, but by the time he arrived she had apparently died. He sat beside her bed, declaring the truth of eternal Life aloud. Her particular work was not finished, and the practitioner told her to disappoint her enemies, that death was an enemy and had nothing to do with her life, that she had nowhere to go because all Truth was present now, and that it was here and now we demonstrated eternal Life. After forty-five minutes with apparently no response, a slow smile then appeared on her face, and she whispered, "I suppose I have no alternative!" The nurses were told to keep watch during the rest of the night, and in the morning she had a normal breakfast. Some years later, she said to the practitioner, "I died in my body. Now I am learning to live outside of my body."

The Repetition of History

"Mortal belief dies to live again in renewed forms, only to go out at last forever; for life everlasting is not to be gained by dying."[5] This is a fact of present, not future, experience. In human experience it is called the repetition of mistakes, which recur until the basic cause, rather than the phenomenon, is uprooted. On a larger scale, the same picture comes under the head of "history repeats itself." Consciousness continues to exhibit the same circumstances, until it, rather than the picture, is changed. This same trend which we can observe here continues. Belief produces the results of belief, and belief alone dies. But the truth is always that I do not die with the belief. The Life that I AM is eternally what it is, and remains untouched by the self-destruction of belief here or here-after. The principle knows nothing about that which suffers from a departure from it. A principle cannot become the opposite of itself.

In this context, we can consider the issue of keeping the horrors of the past alive in memory in order that terrible events, like the holocaust, are not repeated. While, of course, it is important not to forget such things or pretend that they never happened, the real need is to understand that they are the inevitable outcome of a personal, material premise of life. It is that which has to be healed, so that the beliefs of mortal existence are replaced by an understanding of what Life really is. Just rerunning the horrors of the past is not the answer.

Eternal Life

It is not possible to explain death in terms of Life, nor can Life be understood in terms of that which sees death. The fount cannot send forth sweet water and bitter. That which affirms and sees another life, apart from God, is mortality's selfhood, and so is death. That which sees and demonstrates Life is Life itself, with no consciousness of death. Either way speculation about death is a waste of time. The important thing is to get on with understanding and proving abundant Life now. There will never be another life.

Only the understanding of Life removes the penalty of death. The penalty of the grave is loss, bewilderment, and sorrow. The penalty for birth is the penury of mortal existence. There is no penalty in Life, because Life cannot withhold any good from itself. Christ Jesus promised that "if a man keep my saying, he shall never see death"[6] and "I am come that they might have life... more abundantly."[7] The sayings of Jesus all point to Life, not death, as the present fact. In retaining the consciousness of Life, we cannot but be unconscious of death, just as in the light there can be no sense of darkness. The Life that we discern is found to be abundant, because it is all. Nothing in it can be depleted or disappear. Everything in it is new, vibrant, colourful. It is the Life that is God, the divine Mind, in which the limitations and shadows of a so-called human mind have never had a place.

So it is today that we begin to raise the dead. We do this every time we separate our sense of man and our experience from the mortal, or dead; every time we separate, in our thought, the evil, limitation, duality, and temporal from our assessment of what we see and are; every time we banish death thoughts and false selfhood from the consciousness of eternal Life which we enjoy now. There is neither merit nor necessity in waiting. We do not have to prepare for a future Life but are free to "enter into the holiest" immediately.

17

The Knowledge of Good and Evil

...if it was so, it might be; and if it
were so, it would be: but as it isn't,
it ain't.
                    Tweedledee
                        in
        Alice through the Looking Glass

The attempt to explain the origin of evil has occupied the attention of theologians and other thinkers since time immemorial. The assumption behind every explanation is that evil exists. Whether you believe in God or not, you see evil all around you. However you define it, it is the opposite of your personal sense of good and, indeed, of that of most people. Therefore, the thinking goes, there must be something that lies behind and causes it.

One common theory is that there have always been two contending powers, namely, good and evil. A second is that, at some point, original good endowed its offspring with a capacity to deviate from the divine nature and do evil. The first of these observations presupposes an eternal balance or conflict between two opposing powers. The second implies that a cause which is presumed to be infinite good contains at least the possibility of something happening that denies this cause by drifting into evil. Both these observations rest on a personal view of God and man; of God, because He is presumed to include a consciousness of human frailty, and of man because he is believed to have a mind of his own that can take him one of two ways. Only when we see the universe in terms of Mind, or consciousness, as both cause and effect, do these explanations fail to convince. Consciousness can no more depart from its Principle, or Mind, than a rule in mathematics has the option to deviate from the principle that is its source. God, Life, Principle can no more include a will to do evil than He can a will that someone should die.

Relative Definitions of Evil

Perhaps it would not be unfair to suggest that by now all the efforts to explain evil might have resulted in an acceptable answer, if there really were one at this level. The difficulty is twofold. First is the problem of defining evil in terms that go beyond the relativity of personal opinion. It is clear that opinions about right and wrong differ between periods and places. While the Commandments meet with a general acceptance that they are right, good, and necessary for the structure of society, there is clearly difficulty in living up to them. Moreover, customs vary from country to country: practices that are unacceptable in one society are common in another, and certainly the human tendency to seek expediency, rather than absolute good, results in morals of convenience or "locational morals" which will vary widely. The conclusion that is easy to reach is that, on a human basis, it is almost impossible to define good and evil, or right and wrong, in any absolute terms.

Is an Explanation of Evil Possible?

The second difficulty in explaining evil is that the evidence of duality, whatever the dividing line between good and evil may seem to be, is palpable only to the human mind, informed by the five physical senses. And this mind is duality itself. It therefore seems sensible to ask a more basic question, which is whether an explanation of evil is, in fact, possible in the first place. After all, what lies at the bottom of the statement that two times two equals five? The answer is nothing. The only place where such an error can exist is within an ignorance of the truth for, when it is replaced by understanding, neither the ignorance nor the error it includes remains. They have not gone anywhere; they did not come from anywhere; they never occupied space; and their apparent existence was only in the believed absence of the truth. To Truth, there has never been an error, and so it follows that, as consciousness draws closer to Truth, the sense of error dissolves into nothingness. Where reasoning and interpretation take place from the standpoint of the divine Principle, all that is foreign to the nature and character of that Principle vanishes. To Principle, evil never had an origin.

In this reasoning, evil is apparent only to that which does not emanate from good in the first place. It is clear that the human personality appears to be the arena where all the pairs of opposites seem to meet and mingle, and where man seems to be capable of both good and evil. But it does not follow that the Mind we call God can be the source for both good and evil, and thus exist in a state of eternal collision with itself. Ignorance and understanding cannot proceed from the same source. Could it not, instead, be inferred that it is this misconception of man as personality — this identity as a life and mind that are separate from the One — rather than what this personality does or does not do, that is the basic evil? If so, then is it not "the knowledge of good and evil," rather than just one part of this knowledge, that is wrong?

Original Sin

Here we should try to redefine the term "evil" in a more scientific way. Science does not start from the premise of a separate life and mind and then try to draw distinctions between the polarities within it. In Science, the fundamental evil is the belief in this separation between God and man, Principle and its idea, in the first place. This is the "original" sin, because it is the sinful belief in an "origin" other than the divine. Again, we see we are always talking about consciousness, not physicality. Within this original sin the actions of the human personality — both its peccadilloes and even its attempts to do right — are subsidiaries. They are variations on a theme of sin. The outcome of this basic departure from reality is then seen as materialism, objectification, and personification. The first two deny the subjective nature of being, and the third gives this denial identity.

The statement that even human good has its pitfalls is made from common experience. We all know the aphorism that "the way to hell is paved with good intentions." "He or she meant well" is an indictment rather than an accolade. Human goodness, or good on a human basis, could be termed negative right. The wrong in this is not in the intention, but in the fact that such activity is generally in response to the testimony of the senses, which then calls for a reaction. Positive wrong, as opposed to negative right, is easier to define. Positive wrong intends wrong and is wrong, whereas negative right intends right but goes wrong. The latter takes people in more than the former. But the dividing line is still blurred in the absence of any absolute definition. The very practical situation that confronts anyone can be expressed as, "I know what is right, but I have this situation, and daily life does not presume human omniscience." And this is unarguable. Only the true individuality of man, his undividedness from the Principle that animates his thought and action, is safe from error. Steps for good or evil that are taken within the dream of personal existence have no absolute basis. It is always steps taken in line with one's highest sense of Principle that will appear as the highest human right, because they will be the evidence of unerring Mind operating despite, and not because of, the dream.

The Sin and the Sinner

Sin constitutes the sinner, because it is the basic belief of a separate, material, and objective existence that includes the so-called ego that lives this way. It includes the whole educated belief that life is dependent on external factors in any form, and thus that its substance is perishable. Paul's statement, "to be carnally minded is death," might well have been, "to be externally minded is death," for such mindedness is the denial of the true Life and Mind. Externalisation, or objectification, is the basis of sin, because it separates effect from cause and places effect in matter. It breaks the First Commandment to "have no other gods before Me," because it attributes power and worthiness to things rather than consciousness, and so makes idols. Sometimes, within this mindedness, the belief is obvious or bad enough for us not to be deceived. Most people recognise that stealing another's goods is neither right nor intelligent, because it does not make the thief's own experience more abundant. Too much is lost in any apparent gain. But there are more subtle phases of mental thraldom, such as the belief that rest is dependent on sleep, peace on being remote from others, and completeness on being close to them, justice on the behaviour of others, health on physique, and basically that all evidence of well-being is in some way dependent on person, place, or thing outside of ourselves. All this belongs to the dream of material existence. Sometimes it becomes a nightmare, and we take steps to wake up and disassociate from it. More often, it is comfortable enough that we want to stay in it .

The Destruction of Sin

It is at this point of dismissing evil as illusion that we have to be watchful. The human mind is dishonest if nothing else. So merely to know intellectually, or say, that evil is not real, in any absolute sense, is insufficient. Such a statement is of no more practical value than dismissing a mathematical mistake as ignorance, but then failing to replace it with the truth. The philosophy typified by the three monkeys, "See no evil, hear no evil, speak no evil," is moral idiocy if it results either in the permission to indulge evil because it is nothing anyhow, or in ignoring its claim as a presence, and so leaving it for someone else to pick up. "For evil to succeed, it requires only that good men do nothing." The point of either a moral misdemeanor or a mathematical error is that it *is* true to that which indulges it, either by omission or commission, and it remains true, along with its consequences, until the error is replaced by the truth. Then, and only then, is the unreality of evil recognised and demonstrated, and its consequences annulled for lack of witness. "We acknowledge God's forgiveness of sin in the destruction of sin and the spiritual understanding that casts out evil as unreal. But the belief in sin is punished so long as the belief lasts."[1]

Thus, it is important that we define that which is "real" and "unreal" correctly, in order that there should be no contradiction of terms. In so doing we recognise that evil is not real and yet learn how to face its claim to reality. In this way we avoid either an unhealthy preoccupation with evil, which besets much of theological thinking, or the abandonment of standards that is rife today. In Science, reality means all that eternally exists, known from the standpoint of pure Mind. The scientific sense of good is that "no good is, but the good God bestows."[2] Unreality, like any mistake, is that which is perceived from a standpoint that is not pure Mind. The first is understanding; the second is belief. The first is conscious being. The second is the dream. Good, in its real sense, is not found in the activities of the material dream.

Levels of Consciousness

We are really talking about levels of consciousness, so that what seems real at one level is unreal at another. This is why the real sin is false consciousness and why this, rather than the things it includes, has to be dropped. Within the dream, everyone may have his or her list of the ties of the flesh that are to be discarded. We work through the list, if we are conscientious, as fast as practical, and the order of priorities will vary. Within this dream, there will appear to be alternatives, and a choice is made to take the one that is nearest right. We recognise that our own list is long enough to give no excuse for watching or condemning the performance of another, as he or she works through his or hers. And, as we have seen, within the dream there will be no absolute right or wrong, simply because the absolute does not include alternatives.

But the way of freedom from the dream is not by starting from a standpoint of identity with it, and then trying to work our way out. This is the thorny path of human experience. It is by starting with one's identity as Principle in self-expression, and therefore with the fact that we were never in the dream. It is not a matter of the human waking up, but of the human, limited sense of being, together with all its misconceptions, giving place to the everlasting facts of that Mind which never dreamed and that Life which knows no dreamer. The consciousness of wrong never graduates to the consciousness of right. But, by beginning with what is forever spiritually right, irrespective of what the senses are telling us, the double thought of the human mind begins to fade out. Human alternatives dissolve, and that which is eternally right emerges as the highest human right as the mists of ignorance dissolve. Errors fall away in the presence of right knowing and acting as necessarily and effortlessly as steam passing from a kettle.

Redeeming the Past

How do we deal with past mistakes? Always from the standpoint of the Principle that never knows them. There is no merit in letting a mistake — our own or that of another — abide in consciousness, either as guilt, regret, or condemnation. Self-condemnation or the condemnation of another gives continuing identity to evil. Expiation is a poor alternative to the enlightenment that stays above sin and sinner, wronged and wrong-doer. The only way in which evil can be overcome is in identification with that which is ignorant of it. It is in the positive consciousness of the allness of good that the nothingness of evil is proved. And, when proved, what is left to condemn or to punish?

Inverted Good

The sense of the allness of good, and so the allness of the one Life and Mind and nature that are God, is not enjoyed so long as a sense of sin is ignored or retained. There cannot be All *and* something else. We have to face the claim of evil and see it for what it is. And this does not mean to see it as evil. Science and Health states that "the greatest wrong is but a suppositious opposite of the highest right."[3] In other words, it is no more than an inverted view of that which remains the highest right. "Demon est deus inversus," as the Jesuits teach: "the devil is God upside down." An inversion is no more an alternative to the truth than is a negative in photography an alternative to the positive picture. It is the positive seen upside down. The culprit is not the inversion but the belief that there could be a standpoint outside the focal distance of the infinite from which an inverted view could be seen or offered. The belief is bankrupt.

The foregoing brings us back to the basic argument that the definition of sin does not lie so much in misdeeds as in the suggestion that there is a capacity outside God to commit them. Abused capacity precedes the deeds done in its name. And, as we have seen throughout this book, the false standpoint is the human lens, the lens of duality, which nevertheless remains terminology and not an entity. Mrs. Eddy once said of a severe storm that was directly approaching her house, "I looked into the face of the storm until I saw the face of God. That made the storm disappear." True Love, the law of the universe, never loses sight of this face of God but beholds it in every place and condition despite what the senses are saying. To behold the truth instead of the error, the sinless instead of the sinner, and the right instead of the wrong is the sure way to efface the evidence of anything unlike absolute good, and thus leave nothing to heal or redeem. When the light is turned on in a dark room, no darkness remains. "Now a lie takes its pattern from Truth, by reversing Truth. So evil and all its forms are inverted good. God never made them; but the lie must say He made them, or it would not be evil."[4] A true sense, then, of the origin of evil is found in the understanding that everything really has its origin in good.

18

The Study and Practice of Science

If I do not the works of my
Father, believe me not.

Christ Jesus

We must recollect that Truth is
demonstrable when understood,
and that good is not understood
until demonstrated.

Science and Health

A Full-time Occupation

Any science demands a discipline of thought, and any science requires practice in order to demonstrate its truths. A dabbler in science is unlikely to progress far, and what he learns will remain theory unless proved. A musician practices eight hours a day; an artist constantly sees his universe with a discerning eye that looks beneath the surface of things; a research scientist devotes his life to his work. Inspiration is to be accompanied by craftsmanship. There are no short cuts. As Euclid said to his king, "Sire, there is no royal path to geometry."

How much more must this be the case when we are talking about the Science, or knowledge, of being. Everything is now to be seen and interpreted from a totally new standpoint, and its premises tested and proved in daily life. If Science is understanding and the human sense just belief, or misinterpretation, then it can make no possible sense to be shifting from one basis of living to another, or trying to combine two opposite views of one universe. "A double minded man is unstable in all his ways."[1] Shadow-thinking and substance-thinking do not mingle.

"To live so as to keep human consciousness in constant relation with the divine, the spiritual, and the eternal..." is a full-time occupation, just as the practitioner of mathematics or physics must work consistently in accord with the principle of this discipline in order to achieve results. Such living is not to be turned on and off at whim. Both feet must be taken off the bottom of the swimming pool. If this attitude is not adopted, progress will be slow and faltering.

One can note two things at this point. The first is that a discipline is not a formula. It may suit some people to rise early and meditate. Others find that forms of wording help them. Many still find, at least in the initial stages of discovery, that some form of material cohesion, such as a church meeting place, gives them encouragement and support. In each case, the choice of method adopted has, or should have, as its goal communion with God. But the method and form are not themselves the communion. This is found only by *living*, and this means keeping thought in relation to the divine.

Consistency Without Pressure

The second point to note is that, though this communion is the work of eternity, each individual is required only to act up to his or her highest level of understanding and enlightenment. Comparisons with others are irrelevant. We each drop our own baggage as fast as we can, and the only mistake we can ever make is failure to discard that which the consciousness of Truth has exposed as redundant. When a new model comes on the market, we tend to discard our old washing machine or any other appliance that is shown to be out of date. This is just as true when it comes to habits, beliefs, and attitudes. But, when looking at the achievements, or even failures, of others, the only relevant instruction is, "What is that to thee? Follow thou me."[2]

Living in a way that intelligence informs us is right, but to which humanly we are unaccustomed, is where the discipline and practice come in. It is all very well to meditate in the morning, but not so well if the events of the day crowd in and rob us of the peace we found. "The atonement requires constant self-immolation on the sinner's part."[3] Remembering that sin is really objectification, we find that our at-one-ment with our divine Principle is experienced by that consciousness which is immune to the parade of material pictures that passes before the thought. To do this will certainly mean a constant watchfulness throughout the day, so that we are not taken in. It means putting a sieve over thought, so that only that which emanates from the divine Mind constitutes our thinking and animates our living.

A Constant Yardstick

This is the practice of Science. As we do practice what we know, the new yardstick by which we are measuring everything becomes more real, and our assessment of what is "real" and "unreal" more automatic. Few of us have difficulty in noticing a crooked picture on the wall. We do not get disturbed by it, nor do we accept it, because it is incompatible with our yardstick of straightness. We just put it straight.

In dealing with the upside down pictures of the human mind, our yardstick is a mental one, and it is within thought that we make the correction. And this practice, in which we measure the validity of all that presents itself to us by a new, and spiritual, yardstick, leads to its proof. When a change of consciousness appears as a change of evidence, we learn that consciousness and evidence are one. Thus any change for the better is just the yielding of an ignorant viewpoint to one of understanding. This is why Truth is experience — not theory or belief. Only by proving, demonstrating, this Science do we find that matter is never an actual state, but just a misstatement of that which exists here and now as divine consciousness. The demonstration becomes easier as Truth becomes more natural to us.

The practice of this Science involves the constant reminder that the way things appear to be is not the way they are. This reminder may be one's own clear, developed sense of reality. Often, the reminder will be in the form of what someone may say or what we may read. This is why students of this Science read its textbook, which explains its principles and practice. You study to learn, and then you practice what you learn. The proof determines the efficacy of your learning. It is this that gives life and meaning to the words you read.

Tools for Study

One of the tools that students use is the weekly Lesson-Sermon. It is printed in the Christian Science Quarterly, which is available from Christian Science Reading Rooms. There are twenty six subjects only, but the citations within them will be different each six months and will have been prepared by a Bible Lesson Committee. About half of them are concerned with the spiritual facts of being; the rest deal with the theological beliefs about being and translate them back into the facts. The study is a discipline and a reminder of that which is truly going on. This study is not an alignment with any human organization, but a relationship with an impersonal teacher and guide.

In busy times the writer has found it helpful to take even one Bible verse, or one sentence from Science and Health, as a text for the day, and a measurement against which the events of the day can be tested. In such times, also , he has found it necessary to close both his mental door, and also the physical door of his office, just to pause and ask himself what is truly going on rather than what appears to be happening. In other words, morning prayer needs topping up. This was the example of Daniel in the Bible, who retired to pray seven times a day. We are fairly consistent in feeding and satisfying the pangs of the material senses. Far more important is the constant nourishment of spiritual sense, which alone sees reality. Keeping a personal, material sense of things going is a life sentence. Discarding the personal sense is the passport to Life.

The Bible

At this point, it is relevant to say something about the Bible. Many years ago, when the writer was still serving in the British Army, his soldiers used to ask why he read the Bible. The answer was that it was because the Bible was the record of consciousness; that, in it, you found every phase of human thought and the experience that accompanied it. As a history book, of course, it was of little more use than any other book that dealt with human records. But, when the characters and events were translated back into their metaphysical meaning, so that what was written could be recognised in its application today, then the Bible became the chart of Life. This was uniquely the case because the Israelites, perhaps more than any other nation, saw everything in the twin light of human and spiritual experience. Even the names of people and places had both a physical and a metaphysical meaning, and the detail of daily life, in both war and peace, was referred back to "the Lord God."

The Old Testament showed the experience and reward of those who followed the way of holiness as well as the self-defeat of thought that departed from this way. According to the vision of the scribe, the Lord God was depicted as either a tribal Jehovah or, when the prophets were in the ascendancy, as a God who was just and good. The New Testament, built on the teaching of a God who was Love, rather than retribution, pointed to the simpler, though narrower, path of those who recognised the present possibility of the kingdom within — a kingdom that did not have to be achieved by a long march across the desert of hope, nor one that could be taken by the force of human intellect and effort. To such states of thought it was truly said that Christianity was foolishness to the Greeks and a stumbling block to the Jews.[4]

Because this book, or compilation of books, refers primarily to consciousness, its lessons do not belong to a human past or future. Consciousness is always now. The wise man follows this chart of life and imbibes its lessons and so avoids the pitfalls that beset those who are unacquainted with its texts. Remembering the foundational role that the Bible has played in the development of the Western world, we may well ponder the reason for the current climate in which its influence has diminished.

The Inspired Word

It is not surprising, therefore, that the first important point, or religious tenet, of Christian Science is that "As adherents of Truth, we take the inspired Word of the Bible as our sufficient guide to eternal Life."[5] This statement does not imply an arbitrary selection of those bits of the Bible that might fit some preconceived theory. The "inspired Word" can be said to refer to those passages, of which there are many, and especially in the New Testament, that are written from the standpoint of Truth itself — passages where the divine Principle of the universe interprets the universe. Other passages reflect the lesser or greater degree of inspiration shown by the scribe or translator, and the degree to which the pure record is defaced by the hues of his own thought. The Sermon on the Mount is the quintessence of Christian teaching — a sermon that, if lived and practiced by all adherents of Christianity, would reform the world.

The inspired word is effective only as it is assimilated in consciousness. To read any statement that was attributed to Moses or the prophets, to Christ Jesus or any of the great luminaries who followed, as something objective to consciousness, is to forfeit its power. The power of the Word is felt first as consciousness. To understand that the Mind that makes some true and inspired statement is the same Mind, or Ego, that we accept as the " I " of our being, is to translate the words into the power of the Word in our experience. We embody the truth rather than just follow it. Quoting the truth that another has voiced and speaking AS Truth are quite different. The first would externalise Truth; the second is "I" speaking. Without thinking through the words and assimilating the ideas behind them, one finds that no composition of texts is of any more practical use than reading a cookery book and then not cooking.

The Discoverer of Christian Science wrote of her own work that "The Bible was my only textbook." She said that "for three years after my discovery, I sought the solution of this problem of Mind-healing, searched the Scriptures and read little else, kept aloof from society, and devoted time and energies to discovering a positive rule... I won my way to absolute conclusions through divine revelation, reason, and demonstration."[6]

It was the discovery of the rules, or Science, that permeated the Scriptures and explained the demands and the proofs of a life that was in constant relation to the divine, that was then set forth in the book "Science and Health with Key to the Scriptures." This was not written for the Christian Science church, for the simple reason that there was none at the time. It was not a substitute for the Bible, but a fulfillment of its expectancy, as is witnessed to by the countless numbers whose lives have been transformed and healed since Science and Health was written. In the final chapter of the book itself, a hundred pages are devoted to testimonies of the healing of virtually every known disease through the reading of the book alone.

True Evaluation

Without Science, the correct view, which is Principle's own interpretation of the universe, eludes us. Thus, we try to evaluate and manipulate phenomena instead of abiding in the realm of Mind and so maintaining our communion with God. Only Science allows us to evaluate correctly all that appears in our experience, whether it is called good or evil, because we have learned to know and assess *as* Mind itself. In this way we perceive the allness of good and the consequent nothingness of evil. In reality, everything is the divine Mind unfolding itself as experience. Everything is Mind identifying itself and saying , "This is what I AM."

At the end of his career, Christ Jesus was able to say "For the prince of this world cometh and hath nothing in me."[7] This prince had appeared in every disguise — as sin, sickness, death, tempests, lack, hate, betrayal — but none of these phenomena of a mind that was not God could find a lodgement in the Mind that was the "I" of his being . Thus did he overcome them in his experience. This is the example. All that is truly going on is that which I, Mind, am knowing,seeing, hearing, feeling, being, for I and My consciousness are one and All. "The divine understanding reigns, is *all*, and there is no other consciousness."[8] In this consciousness of being, everything is truly as I, Mind, see it, for I see it as it is.

19

The New Heaven and Earth

The divine Principle, or Spirit, comprehends and
expresses all, and all must therefore be as perfect as
the divine Principle is perfect. Nothing is new to Spirit.
Nothing can be novel to eternal Mind, the author of
all things, who from all eternity knoweth His own ideas.
Deity was satisfied with His work. How could he be
otherwise, since the spiritual creation was the outgrowth,
the emanation, of His infinite self-containment and
immortal wisdom?

Mary Baker Eddy

One Universe

Throughout this book, we have returned to the theme that
what are termed Spirit and matter are really points of
view, standpoints of interpretation. The first is the view, or
perception, of being from the standpoint of the scientific
I, or divine Mind. It partakes of the nature and essence of
that Mind. The second, which is the view of the so-called
human mind, is a misstatement of the universe as material, objective, and dualistic. This interpretation reflects the
ambivalence of the lens through which it is perceived —
the human mind. As "I" see it, the new heaven and new
earth are present now.

There is only one universe because there is only one infinite. The material universe *is* that one misstated and misconceived through the lens of ignorance. It is not an alternative to the same universe perceived correctly. This
means that the correct view of the universe, and hence the

186

universe as it spiritually is, is as present as the correct viewpoint. It is not other, prior to, or later than the one we have now. Science and Health states that "sin, sickness, disease, and death belong not to the Science of being. They are the errors, which presuppose the absence of Truth, Life, or Love. The spiritual reality is the scientific fact in all things... Spiritual facts are not inverted; the opposite discord, which bears no resemblance to spirituality, is not real. The only evidence of this inversion is obtained from suppositional error, which affords no proof of God, Spirit, or of the spiritual creation. Material sense defines all things materially, and has a finite sense of the infinite."[1]

It is only finite, personal sense which presupposes the absence of God and so has a godless world. There is only the infinite. A finite sense of it does not change this fact. We have seen that what appears as improvement or healing in material situations, so-called, is incidental to the limited, material sense of something fading out before the true. And this fading out does not result from battling with the material sense, as if it were something in its own right, but by letting it give itself up in our growing understanding of the truth, or that which is. And we have seen that this process is not the result of any personal mind changing its standpoint from one that is material to one that is spiritual. Rather is it the result of recognising that the Mind that always has been ours is divine, not personal. This recognition asserts itself over the ignorance called a human mind and the errors that *it* includes. In this way the spiritual fact that "All is infinite Mind and its infinite manifestation"[2] precludes either a finite mind or the finite forms inherent in it.

Because what appears to be matter is a misstatement and not substantial, this does not mean that we ignore it or condemn it. This is because a misstatement cannot appear unless there is already something true to misstate. This is why "we understand that the worlds were framed by the word of God [the divine Mind], so that things which are seen were not made of things which do appear."[3] The appearance of that which exists essentially as idea, and so as a form of Mind, may be called an aeroplane, a home, a job, a companion, and so on. It could not appear thus unless the form of Mind was already present as the spiritual fact. To interpret this appearing as material is to accept all that belongs to this error of statement, and so the experience that accompanies this misinterpretation, which would involve delay, accident, loss, uncertainty, and frustration. The interpretation of everything as fundamentally spiritual, and so existing as idea in Mind and not an object of sense, means the present experience of all these things in their highest appreciable form— but without the bane that accompanies the wrong viewpoint. Science does not deny matter and then leave a vacuum. It translates matter into its original language (or form of expression), Mind.

A Looking Glass Reminder

The reader may recall the experience of Alice who went through the Looking Glass. At first, she expressed a desire to go into Looking Glass House. Then she went through the glass into it. She found herself in a room which, she said, was almost the same as the one she had left behind. She found a fire blazing away just as brightly as the one she had left. "So I shall be as warm here," she thought, "warmer in fact, because there'll be no one to scold me away from the fire. Oh, what fun it'll be when they see me through the glass in here, and can't get at me." In a certain sense, Alice had learned that the same conditions, viewed from a diametrically different standpoint, brought a new experience — one which enjoyed the good but without the bane; one that was immune from the conditions that attached themselves to the old way of thinking.

Everything good, beautiful, and useful in our present experience presupposes the presence of some spiritual idea. An aeroplane or telephone, for example, *is* the spiritual idea of omnipresence misinterpreted by material sense. It is still an aspect of the infinite, despite the finite sense of it. But the bane that accompanies the misinterpretation of the spiritual idea, called an object of sense, would presuppose the absence and not the presence of God, and so, in a sense, would be a double negative. The misstatement that an idea, or spiritual fact, can be inverted does not, however, make this so. And as the misstatement, or misinterpretation, fades out, the underlying perfection of the idea is experienced with greater clarity.

"The divine Mind, not matter, creates all identities, and they are forms of Mind, the ideas of Spirit apparent only as Mind, never as mindless matter nor the so-called material senses."[4] Matter never creates a human concept, even though it misstates an idea of Mind as human and material. That which is misinterpreted as a human concept is always some idea of Spirit, some form of Mind, that is not wholly hidden by the belief it is material and human. "Immortal Mind, governing all, must be acknowledged as supreme in the physical realm, so-called, as well as in the spiritual."[5] The physical is not an alternative to the spiritual but just the misconception of it. The removal of the misconception does not remove the idea that it misrepresents but enhances it. As we stay mentally with the true concept and enjoy that as the substance, the appearance will be in the form and language that are appreciable, but with a progressive freedom from all that would limit and threaten it. In this way, everything true is brought into human view in its correct light as idea, but not in its incorrect interpretation as an object of sense. We do not deny the fact, only its misinterpretation.

The Appearance Not the Reality

Because all that is true is the scientific fact, and because it is this fact alone that is inherent in the divine, or pure, Mind, we have to be willing to relinquish the appearance for the spiritual idea as fast as practical. When we begin our study, the probability is that the objects of sense are the reality to us, and the spiritual ideas somewhat transcendental. But, as we progress in our study — that is, as the divine Mind progressively asserts itself as our consciousness — the appearances become less satisfying, and often painful. The sweet taste, when the underlying harmony of being is first glimpsed, may be followed by a more bitter appreciation of present experience. It is found then that the truth of the idea necessarily forces out belief in the material object. The young man in the Bible story found it hard to sell all he had "for he had great possessions."[6] His sense of substance was grounded in what he materially possessed, and this was more real to him than the ideas that Jesus was teaching him.

Most of us, in some degree, feel at times like the young man. Human possessions take other forms than just riches. One may take pride in possessing great intelligence, another in possessing patience, another in having good physical health. Every belief that some truth is possessed by the image or idea, instead of by the Principle it reflects, is a misstatement. The realization of this fact seems hard to personal sense, but only to that sense. In a dream, the dreamer may find it hard to let go his possessions. But the consciousness of the true idea is not having a hard time at all. No one, in fact, is asked to give up anything. Many have made the remark that they seem to have more problems to deal with since they began to study Science. The only reason that something appears as a problem is because a false sense of something that is spiritually true becomes untenable. All that is ever true is the divine Mind

190

and its ideas, or manifestation. We are not required to jettison all material things but to relinquish the material sense of them, because this sense, however cherished by time and custom, does not belong to the divine sense of being. Failure, or reluctance, to do this results from the belief that the material sense is the substance, whereas in fact the reverse is true, since matter is the shadow.

Substance Replacing Shadow

It is helpful to remember, in this context, that in reality a personal mind, being without any inherent truth, does not give up or retain anything. The obscure and darkened sense of things that it seems to present, yields as naturally as the darkness yields to the morning light. The light is not touched by the darkness, but the darkness cannot remain in the light. That which claims to possess substance of its own, and that which it claims to possess, are one misstatement and yield together. And the painful sense goes with them. To discern correctly between shadow and substance means that, progressively, we are letting the objective, external interpretation of everything that constitutes our daily life yield to the understanding that its substance is Mind. It is not less but more real because of the true interpretation. The requirement is to let go an outgrown sense, just as in every phase of life we are discarding things that no longer serve a useful purpose, because they have been replaced by new and better models. In practice, we generally do not notice or object when something is outgrown. Friends, social activities, value systems change, and one form drops away to be replaced by another. The necessity of Truth includes the proof that nothing outside Truth is right or necessary.

The only value of an object of sense is that it presupposes the presence of the spiritual idea. As matter, it has to disappear in the ratio that its substance as Spirit appears.

There is no vacuum, but equally there is no room for the material sense as it is replaced by the spiritual. Perfection underlies all that is real, but this perfection is not in the objects of sense. This is why "all things will continue to disappear, until perfection appears and reality is reached."[7] Only by hanging on to a false sense of everything do we find that this sense becomes painful, instead of enjoyable, until the lesson is learned. Paul said, "It is hard for thee to kick against the pricks."[8] The influx of Truth is irresistible.

Abundant Life

The promise of Christ Jesus was more abundant Life. As the dense, opaque, material sense of existence disappears, Life in all its abundance, as it eternally is, is seen and enjoyed progressively with less encumbrance. This applies to every sphere of experience. Old and cumbersome forms of communications, energy, labour have been replaced by new. Life in the home and workplace becomes less physical as everything is seen to exist as forms of Mind. Free from the trammels of material sense, it is found to be whole, harmonious, and perfect now.

"All things work together for good to them that love God [Truth]." Truth, being that which eternally is, enforces itself over that which is not. The spiritual fact cannot be buried in the appearance, nor can the infinite be contained in the finite. In the order of Science, as we have seen, the Principle is above what it reflects. As the divine Principle of the universe interprets the universe, everything is seen in all its form, beauty, freshness, and perfection, for this is how it is. Nothing in the universe of ideas has ever been marred by material sense. Ignorance never touches Truth. Neither the misinterpretation nor that which misinterprets enters the Truth of being. The harmony of being remains intact. Everything is showing forth the beauty, grandeur, and order of its divine Principle. Everything is painted by Love, held in Life, and perpetuated by Truth. No suggestion of an alternative or a threat enters.

The Kingdom Within

This state of true being, as opposed to the misstatement, has always been and always is present to inspired consciousness — to that consciousness that proceeds from the divine Mind. Men and women have glimpsed it, sometimes in a flash, and sometimes in a way that has given them an abiding sense of the beauty and safety of reality. The state of perfection that John called the new heaven and new earth, in the book of Revelation, and which he also referred to as the heavenly city, reached him while he had been banished to the island of Patmos. He showed the present possibility of experiencing the spiritual consciousness of being, in which there was no more sorrow, pain, or death, because "the former things are passed away."[9] In the passing away of the material, objective sense of everything, its pains and sorrows pass also. In this consciousness, too, even the symbols that presupposed the presence of God have given place to the presence of God itself. There were no gates, because no threats, so nothing to shut out. And this true, subjective interpretation of everything included both individual and universal experience so that "the nations of them which are saved shall walk in the light of it."[10] Everything is included in the true view of the one Mind.

Above all, the lesson that John, and others, have shown is that salvation, the millennium, or whatever you call it, is indeed an individual experience. While it excludes nothing that makes up the world of consciousness, it is not dependent on a single external factor, whether called person, place, or thing. Nothing could have been less salubrious than the conditions where John received his vision.

Nothing could have tried to deny more Jesus' statement that "my kingdom is not of this world" than the indignity of Gethsemane and Calvary. Nothing would try harder than the materialism of today to disprove the contrary understanding that everything exists as Mind and its ideas. But there is no need to listen to or give reality to the denial of Truth. The admission of an error is all there is to it, for unless we accept it as consciousness, it has no reality for us. On the other hand, to refuse the denial any foothold in our thinking is to make it recede for lack of witness, and so to deny its capacity to enter experience.

The kingdom of heaven is not a location inhabited by persons and consisting of things. It is a state of consciousness consisting of ideas. It is as present as the Mind we call God. In it, the former things — the sadness and turmoil, the ugliness and pollution, the wars and shortages, the ills and the deprivations — are passed away. They never belonged to divine consciousness, and they have never harmed or disturbed it. This is an unmolested, unthreatened kingdom. "Beauty is a thing of life, which dwells forever in the eternal Mind and reflects the charms of His goodness in expression, form, outline, and color."[11] All that makes experience sweet and beautiful is present now, without delay, in the form and language we can understand and recognise. The only dependency is upon spiritual sense, the correct view and interpretation that proceed from the divine Principle. In the Bible story of Abraham, who was seeking a new country and was unsure where to go, we read how the Lord (spiritual sense) said to him, "Lift up now thine eyes, and look from the place where thou art... for all the land which thou seest, to thee will I give it."[12]

Centuries later, Jesus told his disciples that this same land, or kingdom, was likewise dependent only upon the altitude of vision that perceived it. He said that "the kingdom of God cometh not with observation: neither shall they say, Lo here! or, lo there! for, behold, the kingdom of God is within you."[13] It is within the correct perception of being. It is here, now, and "I" have never ceased to see it.

Appendix

Abbreviations

Reference to writings by Mary Baker Eddy

S&H	Science and Health with Key to the Scriptures
My.	The First Church of Christ Scientist and Miscellany
Ret.	Retrospection and Introspection
Un.	Unity of Good
Peo.	The People's Idea of God
Mis.	Miscellaneous Writings
No.	No and Yes
Rud.	Rudimental Divine Science
'01.	Message to the Mother Church 1901

Appendix

Footnotes by chapter

Throughout this book references have been made to the King James version of the Bible and to the writings of Mary Baker Eddy. The following lists these by chapter.

Introduction
1. John 18:36
2. S&H 107:1-3
3. S&H 127:9-14
4. My. 117:22-24
5. Romans 8:28

Chapter 1
1. I Corinthians 13:12
2. S&H 272:28-29
3. Luke 17:21
4. John 16:12-13

Chapter 2
1. Galations 5:22-23
2. John 8:23
3. Psalms 91:1
4. S&H 476:32-4
5. Isaiah 7:14
   S&H xi:16
6. Colossians 3:9-10

Chapter 3
1. S&H 240:10-14
2. Ret. 56:22-24
3. S&H 390:7-9

Chapter 4
1. S&H 295:26
   409:11
   591:9
   277:26
2. S&H 269:14-16
3. S&H 301:24-29
4. Hebrews 11:3
5. S&H 151:26-28

Chapter 5
1. S&H 552:19-21
2. S&H 109:32-3
3. Acts 15:18
4. S&H 588:22-23
5. S&H 247:19-21
6. Un. 35:24

Chapter 6
1. Matthew 6:33
2. Peo. 14:10-11
3. Mis. 200:1-3
4. S&H 127:4-8

Appendix

Footnotes by chapter

Chapter 7
1. Deuteronomy 6:4
2. S&H 587:5-8
3. Genesis 3:5
4. No. 16:1-2
5. John 10:30
6. S&H 465:17-1
7. I John 4:19
8. S&H 127:4-8

Chapter 8
1. Genesis 2:7
2. John 8:44
3. Matthew 25:40
4. S&H 258:16-18
5. John 14:9
6. S&H 475:14-15
7. Jeremiah 29:11
8. Galations 5:19-24
9. S&H 478:24-26
10. John 3:13
11. Peo. 5:23-24
12. Ephesians 4:13
13. Isaiah 14:16-17

Chapter 9
1. Jeremiah 29:11
2. S&H 390:7-9
3. John 8:32
4. Rud. 1:1-4
5. II Corinthians 5:8
6. S&H 88:9-14
7. Psalms 119:18

Chapter 10
1. Exodus 3:5
2. James 1:17
3. Isaiah 25:7
4. S&H 476:32-4
5. S&H 536:8-9
6. S&H 18:1-3
7. My. 160:5-8
8. Matthew 5:48
9. John 10:10

Chapter 11
1. Exodus 20:3-17
2. I John 3:9
3. S&H 25:31-32
4. Matthew 19:17
5. John 14:12
6. John 3:3
7. John 14:6
8. S&H 583:10-11
9. S&H 589:16-18

Chapter 12
1. I Samuel 8:5
2. Matthew 6:33
3. Mis. 190:4-6

Chapter 13
1. Mis. 249:28-2
2. My. 247:5

Appendix

Footnotes by chapter

Chapter 14
1. S&H 416:16
2. Matthew 7:20
3. Mark 16:15
   Matthew 10:8
4. S&H 428:19-21
5. Philippians 2:5
6. John 12:32

Chapter 15
1. 01. 1:18-19
2. Psalms 24:1
3. I Kings 19:11-12
4. My. 291:10
5. Matthew 24:15
6. S&H 96:22-23
   97:17-20

Chapter 16
1. S&H 371:9-11
2. Romans 8:6
3. S&H 266:30-32
4. John 8:11
5. S&H 556:10-13
6. John 8:51
7. John 10:10

Chapter 17
1. S&H 497:9-12
2. S&H 275:19
3. S&H 368:1-2
4. Un. 53:1-4

Chapter 18
1. James 1:8
2. John 21:22
3. S&H 23:4-5
4. I Corinthians 1:23
5. S&H 497:3-4
6. S&H 109:11-22
7. John 14:30
8. S&H 536:8-9

Chapter 19
1. S&H 207:23-4
2. S&H 468:10-11
3. Hebrews 11:3
4. S&H 505:9-12
5. S&H 427:23-25
6. Mark 10:22
7. S&H 353:18-19
8. Acts 9:5
9. Revelation 21:4
10. Revelation 21:24
11. S&H 247:21-24
12. Genesis 13:14-15
13. Luke 17:20-21